YOUR NAME IS YOUR BLESSING

YOUR
NAME
IS YOUR
BLESSING

HEBREW NAMES AND
THEIR MYSTICAL MEANINGS

BENJAMIN BLECH
ELAINE BLECH

JASON ARONSON
Lanham • Boulder • New York • Toronto • Plymouth, UK

Published by Jason Aronson
A wholly owned subsidiary of The Rowman & Littlefield Publishing Group, Inc.
4501 Forbes Boulevard, Suite 200, Lanham, Maryland 20706
www.rowman.com

10 Thornbury Road, Plymouth PL6 7PP, United Kingdom

British Library Cataloguing in Publication Information Available

Library of Congress Cataloging-in-Publication Data

The original hardback edition of this book was previously cataloged by the
Library of Congress as follows:

Blech, Benjamin.
  Your name is your blessing: names and their mystical meanings / Benjamin Blech,
Elaine L. Blech.
     p. cm.
     Includes index.
     1. Names, Personal—Jewish.   2. Gematria.   I. Blech, Elaine.   II. Title.
CS3010.B54   1999
929.4'4'089924—dc21   98-36488
                                                                             CIP

ISBN 978-0-7657-0967-7

⊗™ The paper used in this publication meets the minimum requirements of
American National Standard for Information Sciences—Permanence of Paper for
Printed Library Materials, ANSI/NISO Z39.48-1992.

Printed in the United States of America

Dedicated to those names dearest to us,
our parents, our children, and our grandchildren

Rabbi Benzion Blech זצ״ל
Gertrude Blech
Simon Wang זצ״ל
Emma Wang

Tamar and Yaakov Har-Oz
Avital Shlomit
Eitan Shimon
Yair Mordechai

Yael and Stephen Lubofsky
Noam Benzion
Daniel Eli
Eliana

Jordana and Aryeh Klein
Talia Yonit
Shlomo Ilan
Adin Zion

Ari Ron Blech

And to all the names we will, with God's blessing, be adding to our family.

* * *

Our grateful thanks go to Arthur Kurzweil who was the inspiration for this book.

Rabbi Benjamin Blech
Elaine L. Blech

CONTENTS

PREFACE

We urge the reader to carefully read the Preface and Introduction before proceeding.

—Benjamin and Elaine Blech

In a rabbinic career spanning more than a half-century, there is one question we've been asked more than any other. Speaking about this with other members of the clergy, it seems we are not alone—this appears to be the single most frequently raised query in contemporary religious life.

Remarkably enough, it isn't about faith; it doesn't revolve around theology. It's something far more personal.

People intuitively recognize the truth of a spiritual concept profoundly rooted in the Jewish mystical tradition. It takes for granted that names have meaning. Names represent our identity. Not simply because they are a convenient way to allow us to be distinguished one from another. Far more, it is because they define us. The names we are given at birth aren't accidental. They are to a large extent prophetic. They capture our essence. They are the keys to our soul.

We believe that words have meaning but names have power. Within them there is hidden the divine core of our potential. In short, our name is our blessing.

No wonder then that the most oft-asked question posed to rabbis today relates to the naming of children: "How should I go about choosing a name for my newborn?"

A name is the most important gift we will ever give to our children. Unlike toys, money or material objects, it is the only thing that will remain with them for a lifetime—and beyond.

Quite a responsibility, isn't it?

Judaism believes that although prophecy no longer exists after the close of the Bible, there is one small area in which we are still granted a glimpse of divine wisdom. It comes to us when we struggle to find the right name for our offspring. Our task, we are told, is to research possible names and their meanings. And as we fulfill our mission, at a certain moment God intercedes and grants us the certainty of a heavenly decreed decision.

The names of our children are the result of a partnership between our effort and God's response.

The book we have written will enable you to carry out this intended search. As you look through its names and the possibilities for your child's blessings, the promise of prophecy will lead you to choose the one and only best possibility.

Trust us: you will know the name you need to select when you see it and concentrate on its meaning.

We say this with confidence in the preface to the second edition because we have had the unusual benefit of hundreds of communications from readers of the first. We thank all of those who have let us know how much having this book available meant to them. Indeed, we now fully realize the importance of our contribution to the once-in-a-lifetime privilege of identifying the soul of every one of our precious children.

There are many books of Jewish names. This one is totally different from all the others. This is the first time that the secrets of the Kabbalah, the mystical teachings of spiritual masters of old, are introduced to the general public in order to explain the most profound meanings hidden in every person's most precious and personal possession—his or her name.

Kabbalah does not content itself with simple translation. A name tells a story: the Hebrew word for name, שם, has the same numerical value (*gematria*) as the word for book (ספר): 340. A name is a book. It captures a person's character and personality. It describes everyone's mission on earth. It contains a prophecy as well as a powerful, potential blessing. It is the only possession we have that remains with us even after death. For a parent, it is the most valuable gift we can ever give to a child.

This book will help you to understand the secret "power" of names. Here you will find all of the following:

- Hundreds of names, Hebrew and English, from ancient biblical to the most modern Israeli.
- A translation giving the sense of the simple meaning.
- The *gematria* of the Hebrew name—the total numerical value of all

the name's letters which is the starting point for a kabbalistic analysis. (See the introduction for a full explanation.)

- An asterisk to denote if the *gematria* is "perfect" or "simple." (Again, see introduction.)
- HIS/HER WORD: The word in the Bible that contains the exact numerical equivalent and links its idea/message to its counterpart name.
- The biblical source for the word which shares in the name *gematria*.
- HIS/HER PHRASE: A description of personal qualities that shares the same *gematria* and alludes to a special kinship between character and what a person is called.
- HIS/HER BLESSING: A prediction about the person implicit in the previous entries—a short, but startling, summary of what lies ahead for someone with this particular name.

WITH ALL OF THESE FEATURES,
THIS BOOK IS FOR YOU IF . . .

- You are going to have a baby and you are looking for a name that is associated with *mazel*.
- You think you know what you are going to name your child, but you would like to know the mystical meaning of your choice.
- You believe that a name is the truest representation of a person's soul—and you want to make certain that you are giving your child a gift that is laden with blessing.
- You want to know more about a person—someone else, or perhaps even yourself—and you would love to discover what secrets are mystically revealed by his or her name.
- You have been chosen to speak at a *simchah*—a celebration of a *brit*, bar mitzvah, bat mitzvah, or wedding—and you would like to associate the meaning of the occasion with the name of the celebrant(s).
- You want to reflect on the lives of your ancestors who have passed away and understand that, according to Jewish tradition, their purpose on earth was summed up in the word by which they were known throughout their days.

TO READ THIS BOOK CAREFULLY IS TO RECOGNIZE THAT A NAME CAPTURES THE DEEPER MEANING OF ANOTHER PERSON'S REAL ESSENCE. WHERE OTHERS ASK, "WHAT'S IN A NAME?", WE KNOW THE ANSWER: NOTHING LESS THAN THE SOUL.

INTRODUCTION

ARE NAMES REALLY
THAT IMPORTANT?

NAMES DON'T JUST NAME—THEY CREATE

Who was the first one ever to call something or someone by name? The Bible makes clear it was none other than God. What is even more fascinating than discovering the author of names is to realize their purpose: Names were first used not for the sake of identification, but rather for creation.

When the Torah says "God created . . ." it doesn't suggest that He worked or that He fashioned through labor, but merely that He said—and the very words describing the object made it come into being. God said "Let there be 'or' (light) and there was light." But how did light know what it ought to be made of? What gave it its properties? What determined its essence? The Almighty merely gave it a name, and the very letters defined its atomic structure.

Ask a scientist for the building blocks of the universe and the response will speak of atoms, molecules, DNA, and elements. Ask our sages, and the reply will have reference to the original moment of creation. Names are not just convenient ways for us to differentiate between objects. Names are responsible for the differences between all things on this earth.

More important than knowing which came first, the chicken or the egg, is acknowledging that names came before the existence of those things with which they would subsequently be identified. Names are not the offspring, but rather the parents of everything in the universe.

Things really are what they are called. Or, to put it more bluntly, they are what they are because of what they are named.

YOUR NAME IS YOUR *NESHAMA*—
THE KEY TO YOUR SOUL

The hebrew word for "name" is שם *shem*. These two hebrew letters, ש (*shin*) and מ (*mem*) are central to the word *neshamah*—נשמה—the hebrew word for "soul." The soul, or essence, of any human being is contained in his or her name.

That is why:

- When Abram came to the realization of monotheism, his name had to be changed: "Neither shall thy name any more be called Abram, but thy name shall be Abraham; for the father of a multitude of nations have I made thee" (Genesis 17:5). A change of identity requires a change of identification.
- When Jacob, whose name came from the root word meaning "heel"—which so perfectly suited someone whose approach to the problems of life was always flight—suddenly realized he had to fight rather than flee, the angel informed him: "Thy name shall be called no more Jacob, but Israel; for thou hast striven with God and with men, and hast prevailed" (Genesis 32:29). A traumatic lifestyle change brings with it a new personal descriptive.
- When the Children of Israel were redeemed from Egypt, the Midrash—the major commentary of Talmudic sages—makes it clear it was in merit of three things that the Almighty took note of their suffering and decided to insure their survival. The Jews may have been imperfect in many ways, but overriding their sins was the fact that "they did not change their names, their language, and their mode of dress." First and paramount was the fact that they maintained their attachment to their "true selves" by remaining loyal to their given names.
- If a person is critically ill, Jewish law suggests a powerful last resort: Change the name of the individual in order to alter the decree. Adding *Chayim* is one example, for this word, of course, means "life." A NEW NAME IS A NEW PERSON.

- It is our custom to name children after those whom we deeply admire or seek to memorialize. To link a newborn with someone from the past is to bring together two souls in an inseparable bond of life.

YOUR NAME IS YOUR CHARACTER, YOUR DESTINY, AND YOUR MISSION IN LIFE

Mystics teach a remarkable tradition: At death every person is asked his or her name. Why? Because your name is your mission. What we are really being asked is whether we lived up to the ideals and potentials given to us at birth.

A name defines a person. Remarkably, the Bible says כשמו כן הוא, "As his name, so is he" (Samuel I 25:25). Talmudic sages offer countless examples of the connection between the names of biblical characters and their actions.

Does that mean then that we are predestined to lives circumscribed by something beyond our control? Are we doomed to play out roles handed to us by our parents while we were infants? Is our free will limited by our names?

Of course that is impossible. Judaism emphasizes the principle of freedom of choice. Yet our names can perfectly describe us because *they are predictions of our futures.* What makes parents decide on one particular name above all others? At a certain moment it suddenly becomes clear that this is who their child is and no other name will do. The decision, according to our tradition, is guided by a divine spirit— one of the very last remaining powers of prophecy to persist even in our generation.

It is not our name that forces us to be what we are. It is what we are that transmits itself in a profoundly prophetic manner to those entrusted with the holy task of choosing our names.

Indeed, every parent is a prophet at the time of naming a child. It is a remarkable gift from God. But it is also an awesome responsibility.

THE SECRET
OF <u>*GEMATRIA*</u>

The most familiar meaning of names is rooted in simple translation. Naomi, for example, as the Book of Ruth clearly points out, was a woman whose good nature was perfectly summed up by the word which served as her name, Naomi—pleasantness.

But there is another method for discovering the inner meaning of a name that is far less well-known. It is predicated on the mathematical science of *gematria*—the calculation of numerical values of letters.

Those who know only English may be surprised by this seemingly far-fetched approach that attaches significance to the total "number value" of a word based on the sum of all its constituent letters. Yet even the English language has words that literate people recognize immediately as being composed not simply of letters, but rather serving as acronyms. The word "radar" no longer has periods after each letter to acknowledge its original source, but of course derives from "Radio Detecting and Ranging." If someone unaware of the story behind the word were to be told that radar can be related to a longer phrase of four words, that too would seem far-fetched. But ignorance of a word's source does not justify mocking parentage once it is revealed.

Hebrew comes with secrets far more profound than the usage of acronyms. The most intriguing, perhaps, and the one often least acceptable to the Western mind simply because of unfamiliarity, is the code of *gematria*. It may appear as a mere game to note the fact that two totally different words, when translated into the language of numbers—for every Hebrew letter also bears a numerical equivalent—share the same total and hence have a relationship. The Hebrew word for child, ילד, for example is 44 (10+30+4). Of course, that 44 is the sum of a father, *Av* (אב), 3 (1+2) and a mother *Em*, (אם), 41 (1+40). It is not simply man and woman, sperm and egg that have merged; it is the numerical essence, the *gematria*, that is as powerful as genetics in the act of creation. And that child, a *gematria* of 44, shares his or her "number" with the word לבבי (ל = 30, ב = 2, ב = 2, י = 10) "my heart," as well as that of the word יגאל (י = 10, ג = 3, א = 1, ל = 30) "he will redeem." The child carries the heart of his parents into a future in which he or she will redeem their aspirations.

Words that are alike in their number total share a deeper kinship as well. That is why we may discover the most profound and "hidden" meaning of a name by finding its mate in *gematria*. As a matter of fact, the very word for "name" in Hebrew—שם—(ש = 300, מ = 40) has a *gematria* of 340 which, fascinatingly enough, is the exact equivalent of the word ספר (ס = 60, פ = 80, ר = 200) which means "book." Every "name" is a "book" waiting to be read and understood.

THE TWO KINDS OF *GEMATRIAS*

A "perfect *gematria*" is the most powerful of number linkages that can exist between two words. It is illustrated by words which share the exact numerical totals because they possess the identical letters merely placed in different sequence.

A linkage of idea or theme for words of this kind becomes fairly obvious with the simplest analysis. Take the word for grave (קבר) as an example. Rearrange the letters and it can become רקב (decay). The grave is the place where the body is placed to rot. But move the letters once more and it becomes the word בקר (morning). Death on this earth is not final. It is replaced by the "morning" of another, far more beautiful other-worldly existence. As the Indian poet Tagore so profoundly put it, "Death is turning off the lamp because the dawn has come." And in that spiritual plane of existence we will at last find true peace and contentment because—with a final rearrangement of those self-same letters, קרב (near), we will have drawn "near" to the Divine Presence itself.

All these words—קבר, רקב, בקר, and קרב—obviously total the identical number of 302. Their linkage, however, transcends a simple *gematria* because they represent the power of the equality of every single constituent part—making them a "perfect *gematria*."

What we dare not lose sight of, however, is the fact that other words of 302 still speak in some way, yet in more muted fashion, to the essence of the ideas contained in the ב-ק-ר union. Note some of these other biblical words which, using different letters, nonetheless add up to 302: שׁב returned, לעבר to pass on, לבער to be removed, אקרא I will call. Death brings return to the source, one passes on to another life, one is removed from this earth, all because God has decided it is time for Him to call a soul back to its original home.

What is clear from this illustration is that the difference between a "perfect *gematria*" and a "simple *gematria*" is merely one of degree, not of kind.

Because this point is so important—and in fact at the heart of the methodology of this book, let us give two more examples before we make clear how this concept will be utilized with regard to names.

The Hebrew word for king is מלך. A "perfect *gematria*" will give us לכם (for you), מכל (from all), and כלם (all of them). These are the highest levels of thematic word linkage. A biblically-approved king must serve for all of you, be selected and approved from among you, and represent everybody. His "number," however, makes his position as well as his mission even more comprehensible. מלך = מ = 40, ל = 30, ך = 20 = 90. Ninety is the *gematria* of פי (my mouth). The king's claim to authority is based solely on his representing the word of God. Ninety is the *gematria* of מים (water). Man cannot live without water; mankind in a social setting cannot survive without leadership. Anarchy, just like thirst, spells the death of human beings. Ninety is the gematria of מן (manna). Just as God provided miracle food to insure our survival in the desert, so too will He appoint those who will wisely govern our people.

For our last illustration, let us look at the very first name to be found in the Bible. "And God said, 'let there be light' (אור) and there was light." As was indicated before, God created by naming. אור (light) came into being exactly as God proclaimed it to exist via its letters. A "perfect *gematria*" of the word אור is ראו (they saw). The rearranged letters describe what mankind is now capable of doing because of this creation. But look at this remarkable list of words that share in the number, *i.e.* "simple *gematria*" of אור = (א = 1, ו = 6, ר = 200) = 207:

207 = זקנים: The elders who enable us to "see" and to comprehend the deeper meaning of life.

207 = הרב: The teacher, the Rabbi, who allows us vision, transcending the ability of the eye to see.

207 = בהר: On the mountain, where God revealed Himself to us and showed us that we can "see" far more than light alone reveals.

207 = ואיקץ: And I awakened, awakened to a higher level of awareness and consciousness in my kinship with elders, teacher, and mountain of God.

A "PERFECT" AND A
"SIMPLE" NAME *GEMATRIA*

Names allow us to discover these same two kinds of *gematria* linkage.

For some names, you will note an asterisk next to the citation for *his* or *her* word, for example: משה—HIS WORD, השם*—The Name (God) (Genesis 6:4). The biblical word corresponding to the *gematria* of the name Moshe (345) is in fact a "perfect *gematria*"—not merely an identical total in number but an exact replica of the composition of this total by identical letters/numbers—the מ, the ש, and the ה merely rearranged differently.

This is the most powerful linkage possible—as indeed the link between Moses and The Name (essence) of God is the strongest one imaginable.

Where no asterisk appears, the name has no biblical word equivalent sharing all of its letters. *But let that not mislead you into believing that it has no Torah counterpart.*

There is a mystical tradition that teaches us that *every person's name can be found in the Torah.* Skeptics have long questioned this supposed doctrine by a superficial scanning of text. Indeed, hundreds of names seem to be missing. Yet, the tradition is sound, if we understand the deeper truth of *gematria.*

Every person has a biblical word linked to his or her name, because there is a word in the Torah that shares the same number total. That word is, in the most profound sense, the key to a person's name. It represents not simply what you are called, but your calling, your life's mission and purpose.

YOUR WORD, YOUR PHRASE,
AND YOUR BLESSING

In addition to the *gematria* of every name, as well as the (Hebrew) Torah word that corresponds to it and serves best to define it, this book also offers a citation for HIS or HER PHRASE.

The *gematria* of the entire phrase is identical with the total sum of the name's letters. (You may check that for yourself by using the *gematria* chart found on page 26.)

This phrase is usually an extension of the idea already implicit in the simple translation of the name as well as the *gematria* word corresponding to it in the Torah.

For example: The very last name in this book is Zohar (זהר), meaning "light, brilliance." (Coincidentally, it is the name of the major work of Jewish mysticism, the Kabbalah.) Its *gematria* is 212 and its Torah word is זרה—with an asterisk alongside of it because it is obviously a "perfect *gematria*," sharing the same three letters with זהר but in a different sequence. זרה means strange, different, and these qualities can, of course, have either positive or negative connotations. Strange can be abnormal or supernormal; different can be inferior or superior to most others. The Hebrew phrase that follows makes clear the positive connotation:

לבעלי סוד (to masters of secrets). The translation led us to recognize a dimension of light and brilliance. The "perfect *gematria*" made us understand that he would be viewed as strange and different—an unusual or unique kind of person. The phrase carrying the 212 *gematria* took us further and permitted us to correlate his uniqueness with a mystical nature and a kinship with those who are masters of Divine secrets.

Putting all these together leads us to the last entry for every name: HIS/HER BLESSING.

Of course it is daring to presume to predict the future. Yet if the name, the *gematria*, the Torah word, and the equivalent number phrase shout out a message of potential, we ought to be wise enough at least to listen to its words and its meaning.

That is why for the name Zohar we conclude with the following for HIS BLESSING: He will be highly spiritual and attuned to the mystical. He will probe the mysteries of the universe with brilliant insight.

Note how the final blessing ties together the various strands of information previously gleaned from the prior entries. Indeed, the שם (340), the name, is a miniature ספר (340) book, of the person's whole life.

Add Your Own Interpretation for Yourself

Don't stop with the blessing that appears in this book.

You are closer than anyone else in the world to yourself. You may sense an idea, a thought, a hint in your biblical word or your phrase, that no one else can perceive.

Think about it. Go back to it often. Consider what it may mean in different times of your life.

No one can do it better than you can. Let your word and your phrase guide you throughout all the days of your life.

But What If the Blessing Doesn't Come True?

It is important to realize that every interpretation is not the same as a firm, unalterable prediction—because the *gematria*, the translation, the Torah word as well as the phrase all relate to *potential and not necessarily to reality*. They tell us what *can be* but not necessarily what *will be*.

Even Divine prophecies, as Jonah discovered when the city of Nineveh was spared, can be superseded by free-will changes initiated by man. The positive prediction assigned to the names in this book correspond to what "ought" to be by Divine assignment and parental prophecy. They are the "ideals" of a person's fate. Failure to achieve them reflects the sad consequence of human weakness or sin.

Do any of the names in this book have *gematria* "partners" whose meaning is not positive? Of course. As the Sages make clear, the Bible itself begins with the letter ב, which, in number, means "two," to indicate the duality of everything created on earth. With free will, we may turn earth into heaven or hell; possessed with almost divine powers we may create sacred sanctuaries or build crematoria and cause untold death and destruction. So too our own personalities are subject to dual possibilities. We can foster the holy or the profane, the sacred or the sinful aspects of our being.

For that very reason, there is an amazing *gematria* correspondence between the greatest blessing and the greatest curse for the history of mankind. נחש, the snake of the biblical story responsible for our expulsion from paradise totals 358 (ש = 300, ח = 8, נ = 50). That is precisely the *gematria* of the word for Messiah: חמשׁיח (מ = 40, ש = 300, ' = 10, ח = 8 = 358). Salvation depends upon rectifying the error of the original sinner. The snake and Messiah are indeed, strange as it may sound, related. They are opposite sides of the same coin relating to the dualism implicit in freedom of choice.

Long before Freud, the Talmud discussed the deeper meaning of dreams, and posited that they often have prophetic power. Yet, when they conclude their analysis of symbols and signs, they make a remarkable statement: "The dream follows the interpretation." Yes, the dream speaks. Its message is profound. But what it says may be taken in different ways. And the way in which you interpret it *is the way in which it will come true.*

This book gives you only the positive meanings of your name. Learn what they are. Relate only to them. Repeat your Torah word, your phrase, and your blessing over and over to yourself. Memorize them. If you meditate, use your Torah word as your mantra.

Dream your dream. Interpret it in the most positive way possible. Make your name predict blessing and good fortune. Believe it in the depths of your soul, and behold, your dream will come true.

USING THIS BOOK

TO FIND THE RIGHT NAME FOR YOUR CHILD

As you think about the name you are soon to give to your child, look over the various possibilities carefully. Note not only how the name sounds, but also which characteristics, potentials, and predictions are associated with it. Does something resonate within you telling you that this is "just right"? Do you feel that the name as well as its *gematria* meaning are what your subconscious—translate spiritually granted prophetic feelings—knows is the truth about your child's soul?

Visualize a picture in your mind of an important life moment ahead and imagine yourself using the name you are considering. Does it sound correct? If you've come to the right decision, you will feel that it is so. Furthermore, years from now you will realize that it would have been absolutely impossible for you to have given your child any other name! Indeed, as our sages put it, the name given to a child by a mother and father is the very one inscribed by the Almighty on His heavenly throne. We, with divine inspiration, are merely allowed to affirm what has already been decreed. It is our hope that this work will make your task somewhat easier.

OTHER WAYS TO USE THIS BOOK

This isn't just a book for expectant parents who want to pick the ideal name for their child. Following are many other ways in which the information you will find here can prove helpful and enlightening:

You want to know more about yourself. Look up your name and discover something about your soul and your "book"—the word we showed you which bears the same numerical value as the Hebrew for "name."

You want to know more about your parents, friends, and loved ones. Look up their names and see how great a correlation there is between their given names and their character as well as personality.

You want to know more about strangers you have just met. Use their name as the quickest "Rorschach test" for a preview of what they are probably like.

And best of all, if you are ever called upon to speak or to offer a toast at any occasion, you can use the deeper meaning of a person's name as the focal point of your remarks. You will never be at a loss for words if you can share with others the fascinating insights about everyone's favorite word—his or her very own name.

That's why we're certain this book will become one of your favorite friends. Please don't waste another moment. Rush to the right page and look yourself up.

FEMININE NAMES

A

ADAYA עדיה

HEBREW	God's jewel or God's witness
GEMATRIA	89
HER WORD	החלום—The dream (Gen. 37:6)
HER PHRASE	ולבה לב זהב—Her heart is a heart of gold
HER BLESSING	She will be sensitive, a dreamer, and a deeply caring person.

ADERET אדרת

HEBREW	A cape, an outer garment
GEMATRIA	605
HER WORD	השש—The fine linen (Ex. 28:5)
HER PHRASE	באר של חסד—Well of kindness
HER BLESSING	She will be sensitive and dependable. She will be a source of kindness.

ADI עדי

HEBREW	Jewel or adornment
GEMATRIA	84
HER WORD	ידע*—Knew (Gen. 4:1)
HER PHRASE	בכל לב—With full heart
HER BLESSING	She will sparkle with her intuitive insight and will be treasured as a precious jewel because of her whole-hearted kindness.

17

ADINA עדינה

HEBREW	Noble, delicate
GEMATRIA	139
HER WORD	והענגה—And the delicate (Deut. 28:56)
HER PHRASE	החביב מכל חביב—The most beloved of all the loved ones
HER BLESSING	She will be fine and delicate. She will be especially beloved.

ADIRA אדירה

HEBREW	Mighty, splendid
GEMATRIA	220
HER WORD	רך—Tender (Gen. 18:7)
HER PHRASE	אהבה רבה—Great love
HER BLESSING	She will be capable of giving great and complete love. Her tender spirit will make her most beloved.

ADIVA אדיבה

ARABIC	Gracious, pleasant, courteous
GEMATRIA	22
HER WORD	טובה—Good (Gen. 15:15)
	באחוה—With love
HER PHRASE	אז אהבו—Then she loved him
HER BLESSING	Her life will be filled with goodness, her years with love.

ADMONA אדמונה

HEBREW	Name of plant, peony
GEMATRIA	106
HER WORD	לעבד—To serve (Gen. 2:5)
HER PHRASE	בכל לבבך—With all your heart
HER BLESSING	She will serve others with complete devotion and find her chief joy in doing and giving.

ADVA אדוה

ARAMAIC	A wave, a ripple
GEMATRIA	16
HER WORD	אודה*—I will thank (Gen. 29:35)
HER PHRASE	זה אבא—This is father
HER BLESSING	All will thank God for her. She will be just like her father.

AFRA עפרה

HEBREW	A young female deer
GEMATRIA	355
HER WORD	בשמחה—With joy (Gen. 31:27)
HER PHRASE	אדם יקר—A precious person
HER BLESSING	To celebrate life with joy. She will be a most precious gift.

AHARONA אהרנה

VARIANT	Arona
HEBREW	Teaching, singing
ARABIC	Messenger
GEMATRIA	261
HER WORD	הנראה*—Who appeared (Gen. 12:7)
HER PHRASE	ענו מכל אדם—The most modest of all mankind
HER BLESSING	To appear whenever needed. To personify humility.

AHAVA אהבה

HEBREW	Love
GEMATRIA	13
HER WORD	אחד—One (Gen. 1:5)
HER PHRASE	בא אבוא—I will surely come
HER BLESSING	To be unique, singular, and dedicated to Father in Heaven. Totally dependable.

AHUVA אהובה

HEBREW	Beloved
GEMATRIA	19
HER WORD	הזהב—The gold (Gen. 2:11)
HER PHRASE	החג בא—The holiday is coming
HER BLESSING	Beloved as gold, her cheery disposition will make every day a holiday.

ALEXANDRA אלקסנדרה

GREEK	Protector of mankind
GEMATRIA	450
HER WORD	מדות—Attributes (Num. 13:32)
HER PHRASE	אשה יחידה במינה—A unique woman
HER BLESSING	She will be blessed with good attributes. She will be one of a kind.

ALIYA עליה

HEBREW	To ascend, to go up
GEMATRIA	115
HER WORD	חזק—Steadfast, strong (Gen. 41:57)
HER PHRASE	אמא חכמה—Wise mother
HER BLESSING	She will be strong, steadfast, and a source of wisdom.

ALIZA עליזה

HEBREW	Joy, joyous one
GEMATRIA	122
HER WORD	כצבי—As a gazelle (Deut. 12:15)
HER PHRASE	הילדה החמודה—A charming girl
	טוב וגם נאה—Good as well as pleasant
HER BLESSING	She will be as graceful as a gazelle. She will charm all who know her. Her goodness will be pleasing to all.

ALMA עלמה

HEBREW	A young woman, maiden
GEMATRIA	145
HER WORD	נצה—Blossoms (Gen. 40:10)
	מטמון—Treasure (Gen. 43:23)
HER PHRASE	טובך וחסידך—Your goodness and your kindness
HER BLESSING	She will blossom forth and be a treasure to all. She will be acknowledged as a source of goodness and kindness.

ALONA אלונה

HEBREW	Oak tree
GEMATRIA	92
HER WORD	חסדך—Your loving kindness (Num. 14:19)
HER PHRASE	אדם בוטח בך—Mankind will trust in you
HER BLESSING	To show loving kindness to all. To inspire trust and confidence.

ALUFA אלופה

HEBREW	Leader, princess
GEMATRIA	122
HER WORD	כצבי—As a gazelle (Deut. 12:15)
HER PHRASE	הילדה החמודה—A charming girl
	טוב וגם נאה—Good as well as pleasant
HER BLESSING	She will be graceful as a gazelle, and will charm all who know her. Her goodness will be pleasing to all.

AMALIA עמליה

HEBREW	The work of the Lord, industrious
GEMATRIA	155
HER WORD	הסמים—The spices (Ex. 25:6)
HER PHRASE	מאהבה ללא גבול—From love without limit
	היא חביבה מכל חביב—She is the most beloved of all who are loved
HER BLESSING	She will add spice to the life of those around her. From her will come love without limit. She will be most beloved.

AMANA אמנה

VARIANT	Amanah
HEBREW	Faithful
GEMATRIA	96
HER WORD	האמן*—The nursing one (Num. 11:12)
HER PHRASE	במזל טוב—With good fortune
HER BLESSING	She will be faithful in her roles as Jew, wife, and mother. She will nurse her children with the milk of mother love and profound maternal care. Her life will be blessed with good luck.

AMBER אמבר

ARABIC	Amber, brownish yellow
GEMATRIA	243
HER WORD	אברכך—I will bless you (Gen. 22:17)
HER PHRASE	בחורה טובה—A good girl
HER BLESSING	She will be a source of blessing. Her goodness will bring much joy to those around her.

AMIRA אמירה

HEBREW	Speech
GEMATRIA	256
HER WORD	ומבחר—And the chosen (Ex. 15:4)
HER PHRASE	נכבד מכל נולד—The most honored of all who are born
HER BLESSING	She will be chosen for greatness, and will bring great honor and joy to those around her.

AMITA אמתה

VARIANT	Amisa
HEBREW	Friend, associate
GEMATRIA	446
HER WORD	האמת*—The truth (Gen. 32:11)
HER PHRASE	שם כאה לך—You will have a beautiful reputation.
HER BLESSING	Her motto in life will be truth. She will be perfectly wise. The sounds of joy and gladness will always surround her.

AMIZA אמיצה

VARIANT	Amitza
HEBREW	Strong, courageous
GEMATRIA	146
HER WORD	המלאכים—The angels (Gen. 19:1)
HER PHRASE	ילד נחמד—A charming child
HER BLESSING	To be angelic. She will charm all.

ANAT ענת

HEBREW	To sing
GEMATRIA	520
HER WORD	רכש—Wealth (Gen. 14:11)
HER PHRASE	מברכיך ברוך—Those who bless you will be blessed
HER BLESSING	She will be blessed with great wealth. Her life will be filled with song and friendship.

ARAVA ערבה

HEBREW	Willow
GEMATRIA	277
HER WORD	עזר—A help(mate) (Gen. 2:18)
HER PHRASE	כל ברכה—All blessing
HER BLESSING	She will be a true friend to many. Always helpful and giving.

ARELA אראלה

VARIANT	Arella
HEBREW	An angel or messenger
GEMATRIA	237
HER WORD	לאור—To the light (Gen. 1:5)
HER PHRASE	כצדיק אחד—Like a righteous person
HER BLESSING	To be a light in times of darkness. She will be especially righteous.

A R I E L A   אריאלה

HEBREW	Lioness of God
GEMATRIA	247
HER WORD	זמר—Song
HER PHRASE	לב הדור—The heart of the generation
HER BLESSING	Her life will be one of song and cheer. She will be the heart and soul of her people.

A R I E L L E   אריאל

HEBREW	Lioness of God
GEMATRIA	242
HER WORD	בכרך—Your first born (Gen. 27:19) ברכך—Has blessed you (Deut. 2:7)
HER PHRASE	לך וה' יהיה עמך—Go with God (ה refers to God's four-letter name, equaling 26)
HER BLESSING	A first-born daughter will bring you much joy. She will always be a source of blessing, and will live a righteous life.

A R O N I T   ארונית

ARABIC	Messenger
GEMATRIA	667
HER WORD	וראיתן*—And you will see (Ex. 1:16) מזכרת—Reminder (memory of) (Num. 5:15)
HER PHRASE	גם ברכה וישועה—Blessing and redemption ישרה ונאמנה—Trustworthy and dependable
HER BLESSING	She will serve as a reminder of your family's past. She will be a source of blessing to all mankind. She will be strong and steadfast in her endeavors.

A S H I R A   עשירה

HEBREW	Wealthy
GEMATRIA	585
HER WORD	העשיר*—The rich (Ex. 30:15)
HER PHRASE	מצא אשה מצא טוב—He who has found a woman has found good
HER BLESSING	She will enrich your lives. She will add goodness to your lives.

ASISA עסיסה

HEBREW	Juicy, ripe
GEMATRIA	205
HER WORD	וצדקה—And righteousness (Deut. 6:25)
HER PHRASE	קול האוהבים—The voice of those who love
	היודע ללמוד—One who has the wisdom to learn
HER BLESSING	Righteousness will be her way of life. The sound of love will always surround her. She will be a wonderful student.

ASTERA אסתרה

HEBREW	Star flower
GEMATRIA	666
HER WORD	ויתרן—And their excess (Gen. 36:26)
HER PHRASE	אז ברוכה תהיי—Then may you be blessed
	כל התורה—The entire Torah
HER BLESSING	She will be surrounded by blessing. Her life will fulfill the ideals of all of the Torah.

ATALYA עתליה

HEBREW	God is exalted
GEMATRIA	515
HER WORD	הישר—The right, just (Deut. 6:18)
HER PHRASE	אין בך שום מום—There is no deficit in you
HER BLESSING	She will be dedicated to truth and incapable of tolerating injustice.

ATARA עטרה

HEBREW	A crown, a wreath
GEMATRIA	284
HER WORD	ונברכו—And shall be blessed (Gen. 12:3)
HER PHRASE	המזל רב—An abundance of good luck
HER BLESSING	To bless all who love her and to live a life abounding with good luck.

ATERET עתרת

HEBREW	Prayer
GEMATRIA	1,070
HER WORD	משלשה—Three-fold (Gen. 15:9)
HER PHRASE	כך יהיה בברכת שלום—So it shall be with blessings of peace
HER BLESSING	She will be thrice blessed. She will be granted the blessings of peace and tranquility.

ATIDA עתידה

HEBREW	The future
GEMATRIA	489
HER WORD	החלמות—Dreams (Gen. 37:19)
HER PHRASE	שמחה וצהלה—Joy and celebration
HER BLESSING	She will be the answer to all your dreams. Her life will be joyous and cause for much celebration.

ATIRA עתירה

HEBREW	A prayer
GEMATRIA	685
HER WORD	תפרה—You will increase (Ex. 23:30)
HER PHRASE	בכל הברכות—With all blessings
HER BLESSING	She will be fruitful and multiply and will be granted all blessings.

ATNA אתנה

HEBREW	Granary
GEMATRIA	456
HER WORD	חאנה*—Fig (Gen. 3:7)
HER PHRASE	נחמד כמו פרח—Pretty as a flower
HER BLESSING	She will be fruitful. She will blossom with great beauty.

ATURA עטורה

HEBREW	Ornament, adorned with a crown or wreath
GEMATRIA	290
HER WORD	רעך—Your friend (Lev. 19:13)
HER PHRASE	ומה רב טובך—And how great is your goodness
HER BLESSING	She will be a friend to all. She will be the epitome of goodness.

AVICHAYIL אביחיל

HEBREW	Father of might or, my father is strong
GEMATRIA	61
HER WORD	מיטב—From the best (Ex. 22:4)
HER PHRASE	ילד טוב—A good child
HER BLESSING	To be always full of joy and goodness. She will be an ideal child.

AVIELA אביאלה

VARIANT	Abiela
HEBREW	God is my father
GEMATRIA	49
HER WORD	ולאהבה—Love (Deut. 10:12)
HER PHRASE	לב טוב—A good heart
HER BLESSING	To love God and to love mankind. She will have a good heart.

AVIGAIYIL אביגיל

VARIANT	Abigail
HEBREW	Father's joy
GEMATRIA	56
HER WORD	בלבבך—In your heart (Deut. 7:17)
HER PHRASE	ידיד וחביב—Friend and beloved
HER BLESSING	She will find favor forever in your heart. She will be most beloved.

AVIRA אבירה

VARIANT	Abira
HEBREW	Strong
GEMATRIA	218
HER WORD	בצלמנו—In our image (Gen. 1:26)
HER PHRASE	חסד עולם—Everlasting grace
HER BLESSING	To serve as an image of the Divine. To always express loving kindness.

AVIRIT אוירית

HEBREW	Air, atmosphere
GEMATRIA	627
HER WORD	תזכיר—You shall remind (Deut. 7:18)
HER PHRASE	בעל נפש יפה—A person with a beautiful soul
	בחיים של ברכה—With a life of blessing
HER BLESSING	To serve as a reminder of all that is good. To be both beautiful of form and spirit. She will be blessed with a special and unique life.

AVITAL אביטל

VARIANT	Abital
HEBREW	Father of dew
GEMATRIA	52
HER WORD	בכל—With everything (Gen. 24:1)
HER PHRASE	יד ולב—Hand and heart
HER BLESSING	To have a caring heart for others and the will to do good with her hands.

AVUKA אבוקה

HEBREW	Torch, flame
GEMATRIA	114
HER WORD	חנון—Gracious (Ex. 22:26)
HER PHRASE	הילדה הטובה והאדירה—The good and gracious girl
HER BLESSING	She will be gracious of form and flesh.

AYA אִיה

HEBREW	To fly swiftly, name of a bird
GEMATRIA	16
HER WORD	אודה—Thank (Gen. 29:35)
HER PHRASE	אז אהב—Then he loved
HER BLESSING	To express and inspire gratitude. To demonstrate God's love.

AYALAH אילה

HEBREW	A deer, a gazelle
GEMATRIA	46
HER WORD	לטובה—Good (Gen. 50:20)
HER PHRASE	ידה הטובה—Her good hand
HER BLESSING	Her life will be dedicated to the good. She will be known for her good deeds.

AYELET אילת

HEBREW	A deer, a gazelle
GEMATRIA	441
HER WORD	אמת—Truth (Gen. 24:48)
HER PHRASE	גילה רנה דיצה וחדוה—Happiness, glad song, pleasure, and delight
HER BLESSING	To shine as an example of truth and justice. To bring joy.

AYLA אילה

HEBREW	An oak tree
GEMATRIA	46
HER WORD	לטובה—For good (Gen. 50:20)
HER PHRASE	ידה הטובה—Her good hand
HER BLESSING	She will be known for her goodness and her good deeds.

AZA עזה

HEBREW	Strong
GEMATRIA	82
HER WORD	עזה—Strong (Ex. 14:21)
	ניחוח—Sweet, pleasant (Ex. 29:18)
HER PHRASE	כבוד אב ואם—Honor father and mother
HER BLESSING	To serve as a source of strength. She will have a sweet and endearing demeanor. She will exemplify a perfect daughter, bringing honor to her parents.

AZIZA עזיזה

HEBREW	Strong
GEMATRIA	99
HER WORD	לאבינו—To our father (Gen. 31:1)
HER PHRASE	ילדה טובה ואדיבה—A good and pleasant girl
HER BLESSING	To enhance lives with good luck. To be a good and courteous daughter.

B

BARA ברה

HEBREW	To choose
GEMATRIA	207
HER WORD	אור—Light (Gen. 1:3)
HER PHRASE	זו מצא חן—This one found favor
	לכבוד אביהם ואמם—To the honor of their mothers and fathers
HER BLESSING	She will enlighten all who love her and find favor in the eyes of all who behold her. She will be a daughter who brings honor to her parents.

BAT-CHEN בת-חן

HEBREW	Daughter of grace, charming girl
GEMATRIA	460
HER WORD	מעשים—Deeds (Gen. 20:9)
HER PHRASE	עם שכל—With wisdom
HER BLESSING	Her grace and her charm will allow her to accomplish much. She will be blessed with intuitive wisdom and common sense.

BAT-EL בת-אל

HEBREW	Daughter of God
GEMATRIA	433
HER WORD	משפחה—Family (Deut. 29:17)
HER PHRASE	יעשה חיל—She will achieve valiantly
HER BLESSING	She will be extremely dedicated to family and will accomplish much with courage and valor.

BATSHEVA בת שבע

HEBREW	Daughter of an oath
GEMATRIA	774
HER WORD	בשבעת*—With an oath (Num. 5:21)
HER PHRASE	קול אברהם יצחק יעקב—The voice of Abraham, Isaac, and Jacob
HER BLESSING	She will live life with the dedication of an oath and hear the voice of our Patriarchs throughout her days.

BATYA בתיה

HEBREW	Daughter of God
GEMATRIA	417
HER WORD	הבית*—The home טובת—Fair (Gen. 26:7)
HER PHRASE	מזלה הטוב גרם לכך—Her good luck caused this פרנסה טובה—Good livelihood
HER BLESSING	Her home and hearth will always come first in her life. She will be fair of face and form and those around her will be blessed with good luck. She will be blessed with all manner of riches.

BAT-ZION בת-ציון

HEBREW	Daughter of Zion
GEMATRIA	558
HER WORD	ובשרים—And with song (Gen. 31:27)
HER PHRASE	בקול אחוה ושלום—With the voice of brotherhood and peace
HER BLESSING	She will fill the lives of those close to her with song and music, and will bring harmony and peace to others.

BAT ZIONA בת ציונה

HEBREW	Daughter of Zion
GEMATRIA	563
HER WORD	לצבאתם—According to their hosts (Num. 1:3) מתענג—Rejoicing
HER PHRASE	היא אחת ואין כמה—She is unique and has no equal
HER BLESSING	She will be a source of joy to all. She will be one of a kind.

BECHORA בכורה

HEBREW	First born
GEMATRIA	233
HER WORD	זכור—Remember (Ex. 13:3)
HER PHRASE	עץ החיים—Tree of life
HER BLESSING	She will be a daring pioneer, leading the way for others. She will be blessed with length of days.

BEHIRA בהירה

HEBREW	Light, brilliance
GEMATRIA	222
HER WORD	ברך—Blessed (Gen. 22:17)
HER PHRASE	באהבה רבה—With great love
HER BLESSING	She and all around her will be blessed with an abundance of love.

BET-EL בת-אל

VARIANT	Bethel
HEBREW	House of God
GEMATRIA	433
HER WORD	משפחה—Family
HER PHRASE	ה' מצליח דרכה—God will insure her success (ה refers to God's four-letter name, equaling 26)
HER BLESSING	Family values will be paramount in her life. She will succeed in all she does.

BILHAH בלהה

HEBREW	Weak, old
GEMATRIA	42
HER WORD	לבי—My heart (Gen. 24:45)
	גדלה—Great (Gen. 19:13)
HER PHRASE	וזה אוהבי—This is my beloved
HER BLESSING	To be in the hearts of all who know her. Her greatness will be known to all. She will be loved by all.

BIRA בירה

HEBREW	Fortress, capital
GEMATRIA	217
HER WORD	ויאר—And it gave light (Gen. 14:20)
HER PHRASE	נאמנה כמוה—Dependable like her.
HER BLESSING	To be a beacon of light to all. All will be able to count on her.

BONA בונה

HEBREW	Builder
GEMATRIA	63
HER WORD	כלביא—As a lioness (Num. 23:24)
HER PHRASE	באהבה גדולה—With great love
HER BLESSING	She will lead mankind as a lioness leads her pride. She will be blessed with great and lasting love.

BRACHA ברכה

HEBREW	Blessing
GEMATRIA	227
HER WORD	זכר—Remember (Ex. 32:13)
HER PHRASE	בעין יפה—With good eye, with generous spirit
HER BLESSING	She will always remember to do kind and good things with great generosity of spirit.

BRURIA ברוריה

VARIANT	Beruriya
HEBREW	Pure, clean
GEMATRIA	423
HER WORD	תחיה—You shall live (Gen. 27:40)
HER PHRASE	אות היא—She is a sign (to others)
HER BLESSING	Her pure spirit will be an inspiration to others and will give her the merit of long life.

C

CARMELA כרמלה

HEBREW	Vineyard, park
ARABIC	Field of fruit
GEMATRIA	295
HER WORD	פריה—Her fruit (Lev. 25:19)
HER PHRASE	חכמה וגבורה—Wisdom and strength
HER BLESSING	She will be fruitful and multiply. Her wisdom and strength will insure her success in life.

CARNA קרנא

VARIANT	Karna
HEBREW	Horn, strength
GEMATRIA	351
HER WORD	ושמה—And her name (Gen. 16:1)
HER PHRASE	טעם הברכה—A taste of blessing
HER BLESSING	She will make a wonderful name for herself and for her family. She will partake of the sweet taste of blessings.

CHAGIT חגית

VARIANT	Hagit
HEBREW	Holiday, festival
GEMATRIA	421
HER WORD	לישועה—For salvation (Ex. 15:2)
HER PHRASE	אהבה ואחוה ושלום—Love, brotherhood, and peace
HER BLESSING	She will serve as a vehicle of redemption for all. The entirety of her existence will be dedicated to the pursuit of love and peace.

CHAGIYA חגיה

VARIANT	Hagiya
HEBREW	Festive, joyous
GEMATRIA	26
HER WORD	כבד—Honor (Ex. 20:12)
HER PHRASE	בטח בה—Believe in her
HER BLESSING	She will bring honor and glory to her family and friends. She will engender total faith in all that she stands for.

CHAMUDAH חמודה

VARIANT	Hamudah
HEBREW	Precious gift
GEMATRIA	63
HER WORD	כלביא—As a lioness (Num. 23:24)
HER PHRASE	באהבה גדולה—With great love
HER BLESSING	She will be a leader with great strength. She will be greatly loved.

CHANIT חנית

VARIANT	Hanit
HEBREW	A spear
GEMATRIA	468
HER WORD	נחית*—You have led (Ex. 15:13)
HER PHRASE	אחת ויחידה היא—She is singular and unique
HER BLESSING	She will always be wise for her years and be a role model to others. She will be unique in personality.

CHANNAH חנה

VARIANT	Hannah
HEBREW	Gracious, merciful
GEMATRIA	63
HER WORD	כלביא—As a lioness (Num. 23:24)
HER PHRASE	באהבה גדולה—With great love
HER BLESSING	She will lead mankind as a lioness leads her pride. She will be blessed with great and lasting love.

CHASIDA חסידה

VARIANT	Hasida
HEBREW	Pious woman, stork
GEMATRIA	87
HER WORD	ויהללו—And they praised (Gen. 12:15)
HER PHRASE	אחד ומיוחד—One and only
HER BLESSING	All who know and love her will sing her praises. She will be unique among people.

CHASINA חסינה

VARIANT	Hasina
HEBREW	Strong
GEMATRIA	133
HER WORD	גפן—Vine (Gen. 40:9)
	מזלנו—Luck for us
HER PHRASE	היא חביבה מכל—She is the most endeared
HER BLESSING	She will be fruitful as a vine and a source of good luck and blessings to all. She will be most beloved.

CHASYA חסיה

VARIANT	Hasya
HEBREW	Protected by God
GEMATRIA	83
HER WORD	והחסד—And mercy (Deut. 7:9)
HER PHRASE	לבה לב זהב—Her heart is golden
HER BLESSING	God's mercy will forever surround her. The goodness of her character and spirit will benefit all.

CHAVA חוה

VARIANT	Hava
HEBREW	Life
GEMATRIA	19
HER WORD	בטוב—With goodness (Gen. 20:15)
HER PHRASE	החג בא—The holiday is coming
HER BLESSING	She will be blessed with goodness and kindness. Her life will be one of celebration.

CHAVIVA חביבה

VARIANT	Haviva
HEBREW	Beloved
GEMATRIA	27
HER WORD	הטובה—The goodness, good (Ex. 18:9)
HER PHRASE	אבטח בה—I will believe her
HER BLESSING	The goodness she exemplifies will serve as an example to others. She will display confidence in all that she undertakes.

CHAYA חיה

VARIANT	Haya
HEBREW	Alive, living
GEMATRIA	23
HER WORD	וטוב—And good (Gen. 2:9)
HER PHRASE	האביב בא—Spring is coming
HER BLESSING	Goodness and joy will surround her. Her life, like the spring, will be blessed with joy and renewal.

CHEDVA חדוה

VARIANT	Hedva
HEBREW	Joy
GEMATRIA	23
HER WORD	וטוב—And good (Gen. 2:9)
HER PHRASE	האביב בא—Spring is coming
HER BLESSING	Goodness and joy will surround her. Her life, like the spring, will be blessed with joy and renewal.

CHEFTZIBAH חפצזיבה

VARIANT	Heftzibah
HEBREW	My delight is in her, she is my desire
GEMATRIA	195
HER WORD	הפסים—Colors (Gen. 37:23)
HER PHRASE	ילדה יחידה במינה—A girl who is one of a kind
HER BLESSING	She will have a colorful personality. She is unique and special in every way.

CHERMONA חרמונה

VARIANT	Hermona
HEBREW	Dedicated, sacred mountain
GEMATRIA	309
HER WORD	ופרחיה—And her flowers (Ex. 25:31)
HER PHRASE	גילה ורינה—Joy and song
HER BLESSING	All her dreams will see fruition. Her life will be one of continuous joy and celebration.

CHIBA חיבה

VARIANT	Hiba
HEBREW	Love
GEMATRIA	25
HER WORDS	יהי—Let there be (Gen. 1:3)
HER PHRASE	אז טוב—Then there is goodness
HER BLESSING	With great love she will create new realities for others, which will gain her great devotion.

CHILA חילה

HEBREW	Strong, army
GEMATRIA	53
HER WORD	יבולה—Her fruit (Lev. 26:4)
HER PHRASE	זה ידיד אחד—This is a unique beloved
HER BLESSING	She will be most fruitful. Her friendships and loves will always be special.

CHULDA חלדה

VARIANT	Hulda
HEBREW	To dig
GEMATRIA	47
HER WORD	לטוב—To good (Deut. 6:24)
HER PHRASE	האהבה וחדוה—The love and rejoicing
HER BLESSING	Her life will be devoted to doing good for others. She will always be surrounded by love and celebration.

CLARA קלרה

HEBREW	Clear, bright
GEMATRIA	335
HER WORD	הצמר—The wool (Lev. 13:59)
HER PHRASE	קול הצדק—The voice of righteousness
HER BLESSING	She will bring warmth and comfort to those around her. She will speak justly of others.

D

DAFNA דפנה

HEBREW	Plant, laurel
GEMATRIA	139
HER WORD	ונפן—And the vine (Num. 20:5)
HER PHRASE	להנאה גדולה—For great pleasure
HER BLESSING	She will be victorious in her efforts and be privileged to celebrate her achievements in great joy.

DALIA דליה

VARIANT	Dalya
HEBREW	A branch, or to draw water
GEMATRIA	49
HER WORD	ולאאהבה—And to love (Deut. 10:12)
HER PHRASE	לב טוב—A good heart
HER BLESSING	She will live to love and be loved. She will be blessed and her goodness will be a source of joy.

DALICE דלית

VARIANT	Dalit
HEBREW	To draw water, vine
GEMATRIA	444
HER WORD	ילדת*—Shall bear (a child) (Gen. 17:19)
HER PHRASE	לנוה שמחה—For a happy habitation
HER BLESSING	She will be fruitful. Her home will be filled with joy.

DANIELLA דניאלה

HEBREW	God is my judge
GEMATRIA	100
HER WORD	ויחלמו—And they dreamed (Gen. 40:5)
HER PHRASE	בחן ובכבוד—With charm and with honor
HER BLESSING	God will judge her favorably and help make her dreams come true.

DAPHNE דפנה

VARIANT	Daphna
HEBREW	Laurel
GEMATRIA	139
HER WORD	והענגה—And the delicate (Deut. 28:56)
HER PHRASE	לילדה הטובה והאדיבה—To the good and gracious girl
HER BLESSING	She will be fine and sensitive. Blessings will be showered upon her because of her goodness.

DASIA דתיה

VARIANT	Datya
HEBREW	Law of the Lord
GEMATRIA	419
HER WORD	אחתי—My sister (Gen. 12:13)
HER PHRASE	נאמנה בכל דבריה—Truthful in all her words
HER BLESSING	A kindred soul to all. She stands for truth and justice.

DAVIDA דודה

HEBREW	Beloved, friend
GEMATRIA	29
HER WORD	ויאהבה—And he loved her (Gen. 24:67)
HER PHRASE	הטוב בה—The good in her
HER BLESSING	She will be most beloved. The essence of her goodness will be known to all.

DAYA דיה

HEBREW	A bird
GEMATRIA	19
HER WORD	אהובה—Beloved (Deut. 21:15)
HER PHRASE	החג בא—The holiday is coming
HER BLESSING	She will be most beloved. Her future will be one of joyous celebration.

DEGANIT דגנית

HEBREW	Like cornflower or star thistle
GEMATRIA	467
HER WORD	בנתיה—Her daughters (Num. 21:25)
HER PHRASE	כי יש לך מזל—Because you have good luck
HER BLESSING	She will set a wonderful example for her descendants. Her good luck will bring good fortune to those around her.

DEGANYA דגניה

VARIANT	Daganya
HEBREW	Corn, the grain of cereals
GEMATRIA	72
HER WORD	חסד—Kindness, goodness
HER PHRASE	היא נאה—She is beautiful
HER BLESSING	Her kindness will permeate all that she does. She will be beautiful both within and without.

DEGULA דגולה

HEBREW	Excellent, or famous
GEMATRIA	48
HER WORD	נדולה*—Great (Num. 22:18)
HER PHRASE	בלב אוהב—With a loving heart
HER BLESSING	She is destined for greatness. Her love for mankind will influence her future.

43

DELILA דלילה

HEBREW	Cord, thread, hair
GEMATRIA	79
HER WORD	מטל—Of the dew (Gen. 27:28)
	במזל—With luck
HER PHRASE	כל אוהביה—All those who love her
HER BLESSING	She will be successful in all that she undertakes. She will always be surrounded by love.

DERORA דרורה

HEBREW	Freedom, liberty
GEMATRIA	415
HER WORD	אחות—Sister (Gen. 25:20)
HER PHRASE	אהבה אחוה ושלום—Love, unity, and peace
HER BLESSING	Her devotion to family and friends will be most important. She will devote her life to benefit mankind.

DEVORA דבורה

VARIANT	Devorah
HEBREW	To speak kind words, or a swarm of bees
GEMATRIA	217
HER WORD	ויאר—And it gave light (Gen. 14:20)
HER PHRASE	נאמנה כמוה—Dependable like her
HER BLESSING	To be a beacon of light to those around her. She is reliable and dependable.

DICKLA דקלה

ARABIC	A palm or date tree
GEMATRIA	139
HER WORD	והענגה—And the delicate (Deut. 28:51)
HER PHRASE	החביב מכל חביב—The most beloved of all the loved ones
HER BLESSING	She will be fine, delicate, and especially beloved.

DINA דינה

VARIANT	Dinah
HEBREW	Judgment
GEMATRIA	69
HER WORD	וכלביא—And as a lioness (Gen. 49:9)
HER PHRASE	לאהבה ואחוה—For love and fellowship
HER BLESSING	She will be both a leader and a protector of her family. The essence of her being will be devoted to love.

DITZA דיצה

VARIANT	Diza
HEBREW	Joy
GEMATRIA	109
HER WORD	מנוחה—Rest (Num. 10:33)
HER PHRASE	גדל חסד—Great graciousness
HER BLESSING	Her life will be tranquil and peaceful. Goodness and graciousness will describe her lifestyle.

DIVSHA דבשה

HEBREW	Honey
GEMATRIA	311
HER WORD	האשה—The woman (Gen. 3:1)
HER PHRASE	בנה הנולד לה למזל טוב—The son born to her will bring good luck
HER BLESSING	She will be the epitome of femininity. Her descendants will bring great luck to all.

DODA דודה

HEBREW	Beloved, aunt
GEMATRIA	19
HER WORD	בטוב—With goodness (Gen. 20:15)
HER PHRASE	החג בא—The holiday is coming
HER BLESSING	She will deal always with goodness and kindness. Her life will be one of celebration.

DODI דודי

HEBREW	My uncle, my beloved
GEMATRIA	24
HER WORD	האהובה—The beloved (Deut. 21:15)
HER PHRASE	היא באה—She comes
HER BLESSING	She will be loving and most beloved. Her presence will bring joy to all.

DORIN דורין

HEBREW	Gift
GEMATRIA	270
HER WORD	רכים—Tender (Gen. 33:13)
HER PHRASE	בגדולי הדור—Amongst the giants of the generation
HER BLESSING	She will be a special gift not only to her parents and family, but also to her entire generation.

DORIT דורית

VARIANT	Dorrit
HEBREW	A generation
GEMATRIA	620
HER WORD	טהרות—Clean, pure (Lev. 14:4)
HER PHRASE	נשמה טהורה—A pure soul
HER BLESSING	She will be pure both of body and spirit.

DORONA דורונה

HEBREW	Gift
GEMATRIA	271
HER WORD	למאר—To give light (Ex. 25:6)
HER PHRASE	אולי אחד מני אלף—Perhaps one out of a thousand
HER BLESSING	She will enlighten others with the gift of her intellect and her uniqueness.

DOVA דובה

VARIANT	Doba
HEBREW	A female bear
GEMATRIA	17
HER WORD	טוב—Good (Gen. 1:4)
HER PHRASE	אב אוהב—Loving father
HER BLESSING	Goodness will be her essence. She will be much beloved by her parents.

DURA דורה

HEBREW	Mother of pearl
GEMATRIA	215
HER WORD	זרח—Shone (Gen. 38:30)
HER PHRASE	נס היה פה—A miracle occurred here
HER BLESSING	She will shine and beautify all that she is involved in. The miracle of her birth will bring joy to all.

E

EDEN עדן

HEBREW	Pleasure, delicacy, paradise
GEMATRIA	124
HER WORD	נדע*—We know (Gen. 43:7)
HER PHRASE	בגדול דעה—With great knowledge
HER BLESSING	She will be a source of much pleasure and joy. Her wisdom will be greatly extolled.

EDYA עדיה

HEBREW	Adornment of the Lord
GEMATRIA	89
HER WORD	יעדה*—Designated her (Ex. 21:8)
HER PHRASE	ולבה לב זהב—And her heart is golden
HER BLESSING	She was designated for greatness. The goodness of her heart will influence all her deeds.

EFRATA עפרתה

HEBREW	Honored, distinguished
GEMATRIA	755
HER WORD	שנתה—Her first year (Lev. 14:10)
HER PHRASE	אשה טובת לב—A woman with a good heart
HER BLESSING	The joy of her beginning will continue for a lifetime. Her goodness will define all that she does.

EFRONA עפרונה

HEBREW	A bird (of a species that sings well)
GEMATRIA	411
HER WORD	טבח—Fair, good (Gen. 24:16)
HER PHRASE	פאר עמך—The glory of your people
HER BLESSING	To be fair of face, form, and deed. She will be a leader amongst our people.

EINAT עינת

HEBREW	To sing
GEMATRIA	530
HER WORD	שׂכרי—My reward (Gen. 30:18)
HER PHRASE	זו מתנה טובה—This is a great gift
HER BLESSING	She is born as a reward to her parents for a special act of kindness. She will be a source of much joy and song.

ELIANA אליענה

HEBREW	God has answered me
GEMATRIA	166
HER WORD	ונקי—And the innocent (Ex. 23:7)
HER PHRASE	הילדה הנחמדה—The pleasant girl
HER BLESSING	She will have a pure and innocent soul. She will exemplify beauty both inside and out.

ELINOAR אלינוער

HEBREW	God of my youth
GEMATRIA	367
HER WORD	ונשׂיא—And a ruler (Ex. 22:27)
HER PHRASE	שׁמה הטוב—Her good name
HER BLESSING	She will serve as an example and be a ruler among men. Her good name and reputation will follow her always.

ELIORA אליאורה

HEBREW	God is her light
GEMATRIA	253
HER WORD	להריח—To give off a pleasant odor
HER PHRASE	בדרך הטובה—In the correct way
HER BLESSING	Her good name will spread like perfume. She will always walk the righteous path.

ELISHEVA אלישבע

HEBREW	God is my oath
GEMATRIA	413
HER WORD	ובתה—And her daughter (Lev. 18:17)
HER PHRASE	שם המיוחד—A unique name
HER BLESSING	She will set a wonderful example for future generations. She will be unique and special, bringing credit to the family name.

EMANUELA עמנואלה

HEBREW	God is with us
GEMATRIA	202
HER WORD	רב—Abundance (Gen. 32:9)
HER PHRASE	בניה ובני בניה—Her children and grandchildren
HER BLESSING	She will have the blessing of abundance. She will set a great example to future generations.

EMUNAH אמונה

HEBREW	Faith
GEMATRIA	102
HER WORD	נחמד—Pleasant (Gen. 2:9)
HER PHRASE	כיבוד האב והאם—The honor of mother and father
HER BLESSING	Her nature will be pleasing to all. She will bring great honor and joy to her parents.

ERELA אראלה

HEBREW	Messenger, angel
GEMATRIA	237
HER WORD	וכארי—And like a lion (Num. 23:24)
HER PHRASE	חברה טובה—A good friend
HER BLESSING	She will be a strong and forceful leader. She can be depended on by all who know her.

ERGA ערגה

HEBREW	Yearning, hope
GEMATRIA	278
HER WORD	כארזים—Like cedar trees (Num. 24:6)
HER PHRASE	דרגה גבוהה מאד—A very elevated level
HER BLESSING	She will be strong and stalwart. She will be ranked in the uppermost level of achievement.

ESTHER אסתר

PERSIAN	Star
GEMATRIA	661
HER WORD	הנרות—The candles (Lev. 24:4)
HER PHRASE	הולך צדקות—Go after good deeds
HER BLESSING	She will serve as a shining example to all. She will seek the righteous path.

ETANA איתנה

VARIANT	Eitana
HEBREW	Strong, steadfast
GEMATRIA	466
HER WORD	ויתילדו—And they declared their pedigrees (Num. 1:18)
HER PHRASE	אשה חכמה ונכבדה—A wise and honorable woman
HER BLESSING	She will live up, as well as bring credit, to her heritage. She will conduct herself in an intelligent and honest fashion.

ETYA אתיה

HEBREW	With God
GEMATRIA	416
HER WORD	וקדשו—And hallow it (Lev. 16:19)
HER PHRASE	מחסד ורחמים—Of grace and compassion
HER BLESSING	She will inspire all to greatness. Her dealings with mankind will be based on goodness and compassion.

EZRA עזרה

HEBREW	Help
GEMATRIA	282
HER WORD	זרעה*—Her descendants (Gen. 3:15)
HER PHRASE	בחכמה רבה—With a lot of wisdom
HER BLESSING	She will set a wonderful example for future generations. Her great wisdom will bring her much success.

F

FREIDA פרידה

VARIANT	Frieda
OLD GERMAN	Peace
GEMATRIA	299
HER WORD	לנדריה—To her promises (Num. 30:13)
HER PHRASE	בחכמה ובידאה—With wisdom and fear
HER BLESSING	She will always honor her word. Wisdom and fear of evil will keep her on a straight path.

G

GADA גדה

Hebrew	Name of plant (coriander)
Aramaic	Luck
Gematria	12
Her Word	חבב—Beloved
Her Phrase	אבא אהב—Her father has loved
Her Blessing	She will receive and give much love. She is particularly beloved by her ancestors.

GAFNA גפנה

Hebrew	A vine
Gematria	138
Her Word	חלק—Smooth (Gen. 27:11)
	הצלחה—Good luck
Her Phrase	מלא כל טוב—Completely filled with good
Her Blessing	She will experience good luck as well as bring good luck to others. Her good character and deeds will serve as a shining example to all.

GALILA גלילה

Hebrew	Rolling hills, boundary
Gematria	78
Her Word	חלם—Dreamed (Gen. 42:9)
	לגדולה—To greatness
Her Phrase	כולה טוב—Entirely good
Her Blessing	She will have great dreams and she is destined for success. She will do and say only good.

GALYA גליה

VARIANT	Galia
HEBREW	Hill of God
GEMATRIA	48
HER WORD	לאהבי—To those who love me (Ex. 20:6)
HER PHRASE	ואהבה וחדוה—And love and rejoicing
HER BLESSING	She will be devoted to both God and man. She will be surrounded by love and happiness.

GANA גנה

HEBREW	Garden
GEMATRIA	58
HER WORD	חן—Charm (Gen. 6:8)
HER PHRASE	וטוב לה—And good for her
HER BLESSING	She will not only be charming, but she will lead a charmed life as well. She will succeed in all her endeavors.

GANIT גנית

HEBREW	Defender
GEMATRIA	463
HER WORD	חבונה—Wisdom, understanding (Deut. 32:28)
HER PHRASE	לעושׂה לטובה—To do for good
HER BLESSING	Her understanding will allow her to overcome all obstacles. Her goals will be reached through her good deeds.

GARNIT גרנית

HEBREW	Granary
GEMATRIA	663
HER WORD	זמירות—Songs
HER PHRASE	החכמה עתיקה—The ancient wisdom
HER BLESSING	Her life will be filled with joyous sounds. She learns well from the lessons of her forebears.

GAVRIELA גבריאלה

VARIANT	Gabriela
HEBREW	Heroine, strong
GEMATRIA	251
HER WORD	המראה—The appearance (Gen. 41:4)
HER PHRASE	כי יבנה ויצליח—Because she will build and succeed
HER BLESSING	Her appearance and her actions will be pleasing to all. Her goals will be reached successfully.

GAYORA גיורה

VARIANT	Giora
HEBREW	Valley of light
GEMATRIA	224
HER WORD	הטהרה—The pure (Gen. 8:20)
HER PHRASE	קול מלא טוב—A sound full of goodness
HER BLESSING	She will be pure of soul and spirit. She will be surrounded with the sights and sounds of good deeds.

GAZIT גזית

HEBREW	Hewn stone
GEMATRIA	420
HER WORD	שלמים—Peaceful (Gen. 34:21)
HER PHRASE	חיים של טובה—A life of goodness
HER BLESSING	The pursuit of peace will be a lifetime goal. Her life will be dedicated to goodness and charity.

GEULA גאולה

VARIANT	Geulah
HEBREW	Redemption
GEMATRIA	45
HER WORD	אדם—Mankind, humanity (Gen. 1:26)
HER PHRASE	ידיד טוב—A beloved friend
HER BLESSING	She will bring great credit to her family and all mankind. Her devotion to family and friends will bring them great joy.

GEVIRA גבירה

HEBREW	Powerful ruler, lady, queen
GEMATRIA	220
HER WORD	טהור—Pure (Ex. 25:11)
HER PHRASE	חביב לנו מכל חביב—More beloved to us than others we love
HER BLESSING	The purity of her thoughts will translate into purity of actions. Her endearing qualities will make her the most beloved of all.

GIBORA גיבורה

VARIANT	Givora
HEBREW	Strong, heroine
GEMATRIA	226
HER WORD	ורדו—And have dominion (Gen. 1:28)
HER PHRASE	להצלחה גדולה—To great success
HER BLESSING	She will possess qualities of leadership. The paths she chooses will insure success in her endeavors.

GILA גילה

VARIANT	Gilah
HEBREW	Joy
GEMATRIA	48
HER WORD	לאהבי—To those who love me (Ex. 20:6)
HER PHRASE	ואהבה וחדוה—And love and rejoicing
HER BLESSING	She will be devoted to both God and man. She will be surrounded by love and happiness.

GILADA גלעדה

HEBREW	Joy is forever, the hill is my witness
GEMATRIA	112
HER WORD	לבניך—To your children (Ex. 34:16)
HER PHRASE	לכבוד אב ואם—To the honor of father and mother
HER BLESSING	She will set a wonderful example for her children to follow. She will bring great credit and honor to all.

GIMRA גמרה

HEBREW	To ripen, fulfill, complete
GEMATRIA	248
HER WORD	וברכך—And bless you (Deut. 7:31)
HER PHRASE	בדרך טובה—In a good way
HER BLESSING	She will be a source of blessing to her family and friends. She will always choose the righteous path.

GINA גינה

VARIANT	Gena
HEBREW	Garden
GEMATRIA	68
HER WORD	ינהג*—Will lead (Deut. 4:27)
HER PHRASE	כי היא טובה—Because she is good
HER BLESSING	She is destined to be a leader among mankind. She will succeed in all that she attempts because of her innate goodness.

GINAS גינת

VARIANT	Ginat
HEBREW	Garden
GEMATRIA	463
HER WORD	תבונה—Wisdom, understanding (Deut. 32:28)
HER PHRASE	לעושה לטובה—To do for good
HER BLESSING	Her understanding will allow her to overcome all obstacles. Her goals will be reached through her good deeds.

GISA גיזה

VARIANT	Giza
HEBREW	Cut stone, cut wool
GEMATRIA	25
HER WORD	ובטוב—And with goodness (Deut. 28:47)
HER PHRASE	אז טוב—Then will be good
HER BLESSING	With the goodness of her heart she will win over everyone. She will devote her life to the pursuit of goodness.

GIVA גבעה

HEBREW	A high place or hill
GEMATRIA	80
HER WORD	בחלם—In a dream (Gen. 20:6)
HER PHRASE	גדול כבודה—Great is her honor
HER BLESSING	The reality of her life will exceed all dreams for her future. She will be greatly honored.

GOMER גומר

HEBREW	To complete, finish
GEMATRIA	249
HER WORD	הצדיקים—The righteous (Gen. 18:28)
HER PHRASE	נאמן ונחמד—Trustworthy and charming
HER BLESSING	She will be among the righteous who do only good. She will be known for her charming nature and her truthful behavior.

GOZALA גוזלה

HEBREW	Young bird
GEMATRIA	51
HER WORD	אמי—My mother (Gen. 20:12)
HER PHRASE	טוב כזהב—Good as gold
HER BLESSING	Her family will always be an important factor in her life. She will set a shining example.

GURICE גורית

VARIANT	Gurit
HEBREW	The young of an animal
GEMATRIA	619
HER WORD	בריאות—Healthy (Gen. 41:5)
HER PHRASE	כי מצאת חן—Because you found favor
HER BLESSING	She will be healthy of mind and body. She will be pleasing to all.

H

HADAR הדר

HEBREW	Splendor, glory
GEMATRIA	209
HER WORD	רדה*—Descend (Gen. 45:9)
HER PHRASE	לבעל מזל—For a master of *mazal* (good fortune)
HER BLESSING	Every seeming time of descent is but an opportunity for her to rise even higher with her special gift of good fortune.

HADARA הדרה

VARIANT	Hadera
HEBREW	Beautiful, ornamented, honored
GEMATRIA	214
HER WORD	ויצחק—And laughed (Gen. 17:17)
HER PHRASE	קול החכמה—The voice of wisdom
HER BLESSING	Laughter and joy will always be an important part of her life. She will always act with wisdom as well as common sense.

HADAS הדס

HEBREW	Myrtle
GEMATRIA	69
HER WORD	אבינו—Our father (Gen. 19:31)
HER PHRASE	לאהבה ואחוה—For love and brotherhood
HER BLESSING	She will be extremely devoted to her family, her parents, her siblings, and her own children.

HADASSAH הדסה

HEBREW	A myrtle tree
GEMATRIA	74
HER WORD	לבבם—To their heart (Lev. 26:41)
HER PHRASE	טוב מטוב—Good of the good
HER BLESSING	She will touch the hearts of all who know her. She will excel in all that she undertakes.

HAGAR הגר

HEBREW	Stranger, emigration
GEMATRIA	208
HER WORD	יצחק—Will laugh (Gen. 21:6)
HER PHRASE	נחמו נחמו—A double comfort
HER BLESSING	She will bring laughter to all and serve as a source of comfort.

HERTZLIYA הרצליה

HEBREW	City in Israel named for Theodore Herzl
GEMATRIA	340
HER WORD	מפרך—I will make you fruitful (Gen. 48:4)
HER PHRASE	רק טוב ואדיב—Only good and pleasant
HER BLESSING	Her ideas will always bear fruit. Her good and pleasant demeanor will endear her to all.

HILA הלה

HEBREW	Praise
GEMATRIA	40
HER WORD	ובלב—And in the heart (Ex. 31:6)
HER PHRASE	טוב ואדיב—Good and pleasant
HER BLESSING	Her good heart will endear her to all. Her pleasing manner will ensure success in all her endeavors.

HODAYA הודיה

HEBREW	Praise, thanksgiving
GEMATRIA	30
HER WORD	יהודה*—Judah (Gen. 29:35)
HER PHRASE	ביד זהב—With golden hand
HER BLESSING	Her grateful spirit and her golden abilities will endear her to others and make her a born leader.

I

IDIT עידית

HEBREW	Elite, best
GEMATRIA	494
HER WORD	ידעתי*—I know (Gen. 4:9)
HER PHRASE	כל מעשה ידיה—All the works of her hands
HER BLESSING	Her superior intelligence will be evident in all the works of her hands and she will be acknowledged as one of the elite.

ILANA אילנה

VARIANT	Elana
HEBREW	A tree
GEMATRIA	96
HER WORD	המלאך—The angel (Gen. 48:16)
HER PHRASE	במזל טוב—With good luck
HER BLESSING	Her angelic behavior and winning ways will make her most beloved. She will be successful in all her endeavors.

ILIT עילית

HEBREW	Elite
GEMATRIA	520
HER WORD	רכש—Wealth (Gen. 14:11)
HER PHRASE	אברכה מברכיך—I will bless those who bless you
HER BLESSING	She will stand head and shoulders above others and be especially blessed with talents and wealth.

63

ILLA עילה

ARAMAIC	Uppermost, superlative
GEMATRIA	115
HER WORD	יעלה*—Will go up, ascend (Gen. 2:6)
HER PHRASE	אהבה ללא גבול—Boundless love
HER BLESSING	She will be a perfectionist who will excel in all things.

IMMA אמא

HEBREW	Mother
GEMATRIA	42
HER WORD	לבי—My heart (Gen. 24:45)
	גדלה—Great (Gen. 19:13)
HER PHRASE	וזה אוהבי—And this is my beloved
HER BLESSING	To be in your heart and in the hearts of all who know her. Her greatness will be acknowledged and she will be loved by all.

INBAL ענבל

HEBREW	Clapper, tongue of bell
GEMATRIA	152
HER WORD	והמצוה—And the commandment (Ex. 24:12)
HER PHRASE	עין טובה—A good eye, a generous nature
HER BLESSING	Kind and compassionate, she will be the bearer of good tidings and the doer of good deeds.

IRIS עירית

VARIANT	Irit
HEBREW	Name of a flower
GEMATRIA	690
HER WORD	תמרים—Palm trees (Ex. 15:27)
HER PHRASE	חכמה ותורה—Wisdom and Torah
HER BLESSING	All her endeavors will reach successful fruition. She will behave both wisely and spiritually.

ITI   אתי

VARIANT	Itti
HEBREW	With me
GEMATRIA	411
HER WORD	טבח—Fair, good (Gen. 24:16)
HER PHRASE	פאר עמך—The glory of your people
HER BLESSING	To be fair of face, form, and deed. She will be a leader among our people.

IVRI   עברי

HEBREW	From the other side
GEMATRIA	282
HER WORD	זרעה—Her descendants (Gen. 3:15)
HER PHRASE	בחכמה רבה—With a lot of wisdom
HER BLESSING	She will set a wonderful example for future generations. Her great wisdom will bring her much success.

K

KALANIT כלנית

VARIANT	Calanit
HEBREW	Name of an Israeli wildflower
GEMATRIA	510
HER WORD	שרי—Princes, rulers (Gen. 47:7)
HER PHRASE	כי אין כמוה בכל הארץ—Because there is no one like her in all the land
HER BLESSING	She will be a superior person who will set an example for others. She will be a very unique and successful individual.

KANIT קנית

HEBREW	Songbird
GEMATRIA	560
HER WORD	ישרים—Righteous ones (Num. 23:10)
HER PHRASE	גמילת החסד—The expression of acts of kindness
HER BLESSING	She will be dedicated to doing good and—like a bird of song—will bring cheer to others.

KARMA כרמה

VARIANT	Carma
HEBREW	Vineyard
GEMATRIA	265
HER WORD	נאדרי—Glorious (Ex. 15:6)
HER PHRASE	פעמים באהבה—Two times with love
HER BLESSING	Her future will take her along a glorious path. She will be most beloved and doubly blessed.

KARNIELA קרניאלה

VARIANT	Carniela
HEBREW	Horn of the Lord
GEMATRIA	396
HER WORD	ושמים—And heaven (Gen. 2:4)
HER PHRASE	גם בין אדם לחברו—Also between man and man
HER BLESSING	She will set high goals and achieve greatness. She will observe both obligations to her fellow man as well as to the heavens.

KEDMA קדמה

HEBREW	Towards the East
GEMATRIA	149
HER WORD	והצליח—And prospers (Gen. 24:40)
HER PHRASE	הידיד היחיד והמיוחד—The beloved one, special, and unique
HER BLESSING	She will prosper in all that she undertakes. She will be a most unique friend and lover.

KEFIRA כפירה

HEBREW	A young lioness
GEMATRIA	315
HER WORD	חשבה—Meant (Gen. 50:20)
HER PHRASE	לטובה ולברכה—For good and for blessing
HER BLESSING	Her thoughts will be firm and bold. Her actions will bring both joy and blessing to all.

KELILA כלילה

HEBREW	A crown
GEMATRIA	95
HER WORD	יפה—Beautiful (Gen. 12:14)
HER PHRASE	יגל לבך—Your heart will rejoice
HER BLESSING	She will have a wonderful influence on the hearts of others, making them rejoice. Her beauty will crown her with regal authority and bearing.

KEREN קֶרֶן

VARIANT	Karen
HEBREW	Horn of an animal
GEMATRIA	350
HER WORD	שכל—Guided wisely (Gen. 48:14)
HER PHRASE	קול דודי דופק—The voice of my beloved calls out
HER BLESSING	She will live an intelligent life and will lead others with her wisdom. The sounds of love will always surround her.

KERET קֶרֶת

HEBREW	City or settlement
GEMATRIA	700
HER WORD	פרכת—Veil, partition (Ex. 26:31)
HER PHRASE	צדיק ותמים—Holy and pure
HER BLESSING	She will know how to overlook the failings of others and to judge them favorably. She will be holy and pure of spirit.

KESHET קֶשֶׁת

HEBREW	A rainbow
GEMATRIA	800
HER WORD	תת—Give (Gen. 4:12)
HER PHRASE	שמחת לבך—The joy of your heart
HER BLESSING	She will have a very loving and giving nature, bringing joy to all those around her.

KESHISHA קְשִׁישָׁה

ARAMAIC	Old, elder
GEMATRIA	715
HER WORD	וקטרת—And the incense (Num. 4:16)
HER PHRASE	ביתה מלא ברכה—Her house is full of blessing
HER BLESSING	Like wondrous perfume, she will make sweet her surroundings. She will be a source of blessing to her family and friends.

KETIFA קטיפה

ARABIC	To pluck, velvet
GEMATRIA	204
HER WORD	צדיק—Righteous (Gen. 6:9)
HER PHRASE	קול חכם—The voice of a wise person
HER BLESSING	She will be righteous, honorable, and have a voice of wisdom. Her ways will be smooth as velvet.

KETZIA קציעה

VARIANTS	Kassia, Cassia
HEBREW	Fragrant, powdered cinnamon-like bark
GEMATRIA	275
HER WORD	ונדריה—And her vows (Num. 30:7)
HER PHRASE	היא נאמנה ונחמדה—She is trustworthy and charming
HER BLESSING	She will be a woman of her word. She will always be dependable.

KINNERET כנרת

HEBREW	Harp
GEMATRIA	670
HER WORD	שלשם—Day before yesterday (Gen. 31:5)
HER PHRASE	גם חיים של ברכה—Also with a life of blessing
HER BLESSING	Her past will be the foundation upon which she will build a successful future. Her life will be filled with joy and she will also be a source of blessing to those around her.

KITRA כתרה

HEBREW	Crown
GEMATRIA	625
HER WORD	כאדרת—Like a mantle (Gen. 25:25)
HER PHRASE	חיים של ברכה—A life of blessing
HER BLESSING	Her dignity will surround her. Her life will be one of blessing.

KOCHAVA כוכבה

VARIANT	Cochava
HEBREW	Star
GEMATRIA	53
HER WORD	יבולה—Her fruit (Lev. 26:4)
HER PHRASE	זה ידיד אחד—This is a unique beloved
HER BLESSING	She will be most fruitful. Her friendships and loves will be special.

KORENET קורנת

VARIANT	Corenet
HEBREW	To shine, to emit rays
GEMATRIA	756
HER WORD	ותרצני—And you were pleased with me (Gen. 33:10)
HER PHRASE	רוח חכמה ותבונה—Spirit of wisdom and understanding
HER BLESSING	She will be pleasing both to God and man. Her wisdom and understanding will endear her to all.

L

LAILA לילה

VARIANT	Leila
HEBREW	Nocturnal, night, dark-haired
GEMATRIA	75
HER WORD	בחכמה—In wisdom (Ex. 31:3)
HER PHRASE	לב גדול—A big heart
HER BLESSING	She will be wise and have a loving and generous heart.

LEAH לאה

VARIANT	Leya
HEBREW	To be weary
GEMATRIA	36
HER WORD	היטיב—He dealt well (Gen. 12:16)
HER PHRASE	וטובה באה—And good is coming
HER BLESSING	She is God's blessing to us even and especially in times of darkness. She will be a vehicle for good.

LEE לי

HEBREW	To me
GEMATRIA	40
HER WORD	חלב—The fat, the best (Gen. 45:18)
HER PHRASE	אך בטוב—Only with goodness
HER BLESSING	With goodness and generosity, she will offer sacrifices of her time and possession to everyone in need.

LEEAT ליאת

VARIANT	Liat
HEBREW	You are mine
GEMATRIA	441
HER WORD	אמת—Truth (Gen. 24:48)
HER PHRASE	למנהיג הצבור—For a leader of the community
HER BLESSING	She will be dedicated to truth. She will be appointed a leader of her people.

LENA לינה

HEBREW	To dwell, sleep
GEMATRIA	95
HER WORD	יפה—Beautiful (Gen. 39:6)
HER PHRASE	טוב וחסד—Good and kind
HER BLESSING	She will be beautiful inside and out. She will always act in a good and just manner.

LEONA ליאונה

HEBREW	My strength
GEMATRIA	102
HER WORD	נחמד—Pleasant (Gen. 2:9)
HER PHRASE	חיים בכבוד—Life with honor
HER BLESSING	Her pleasant nature will serve as chief of her strengths insuring her honor and respect throughout her days.

LEORA ליאורה

VARIANT	Liora
HEBREW	Light, my light
GEMATRIA	252
HER WORD	לברך—To bless (Gen. 27:30)
HER PHRASE	לב טהור—A pure heart
HER BLESSING	She will always be a source of joy and blessing to all. She will be pure of heart and soul.

LETIFA לטיפה

VARIANT	Letipha
HEBREW	Caress
GEMATRIA	134
HER WORD	והענינ—And delicate (Deut. 28:54)
HER PHRASE	לב מבין—An understanding heart
HER BLESSING	She will be dainty and delicate of face and form. Her understanding heart will endear her to all.

LEVANAH לבנה

HEBREW	White, the moon
GEMATRIA	87
HER WORD	ויהללו—And they praised (Gen. 12:15)
HER PHRASE	אחד ומיוחד—One and only
HER BLESSING	All who know and love her will sing her praises. She will be unique.

LEVIA לויה

VARIANT	Livia
HEBREW	To join
GEMATRIA	51
HER WORD	אמי—My mother (Gen. 20:12)
HER PHRASE	טוב כזהב—Good as gold
HER BLESSING	Her family will always be an important factor in her life. She will set a shining example.

LIBA ליבה

VARIANTS	Leba, Lieba
YIDDISH	Loved one
GEMATRIA	47
HER WORD	לטוב—To good (Deut. 6:24)
HER PHRASE	האהבה וחדוה—The love and rejoicing
HER BLESSING	Her life will be devoted to doing good for others. She will be surrounded by love and rejoicing.

LILY לילי

HEBREW	Name of flower
GEMATRIA	80
HER WORD	בחלם—In a dream (Gen. 20:6)
HER PHRASE	גדול כבודה—Great is her honor
HER BLESSING	The reality of her life will exceed all dreams for her future. She will be extremely honored.

LIRIT לירית

HEBREW	Musical, poetic, lyrical
GEMATRIA	650
HER WORD	תרים—Turtle doves (Lev. 5:7)
HER PHRASE	לנשמה טהורה—For a pure soul
HER BLESSING	She will always be a symbol of love and peace. The purity of her soul will be an example to all.

LIRONA לירונה

HEBREW	Song is mine
GEMATRIA	301
HER WORD	אש—Fire, torch (Gen. 16:17)
HER PHRASE	היא זכורה לטוב—She will be remembered for her goodness
HER BLESSING	She will light the fire of truth and justice with passion. Her reputation for good deeds will both precede her and be remembered afterwards.

LITAL ליטל

HEBREW	Dew is mine
GEMATRIA	79
HER WORD	מטל—Of the dew (Gen. 27:28) במזל—With luck
HER PHRASE	כל אוהבה—All those who love her
HER BLESSING	She will be successful in all that she undertakes. She will always be surrounded by love.

LIVIA לביאה

VARIANT	Liviya
HEBREW	Lioness
GEMATRIA	48
HER WORD	לאהבי*—To those who love me (Ex. 20:6)
HER PHRASE	ואהבה וחדוה—And love and rejoicing
HER BLESSING	She will be devoted to both God and man. She will be surrounded by love and happiness.

M

MAGAL מגל

HEBREW	Scythe
GEMATRIA	73
HER WORD	החיים—The life (Gen. 2:9)
HER PHRASE	זה היום—This very day
HER BLESSING	She will never delay her good deeds. She will harvest the fruits of her acts of kindness.

MAHIRA מהירה

VARIANT	Mehira
HEBREW	Speedy, energetic
GEMATRIA	260
HER WORD	ירים—Raise up (Gen. 41:44)
HER PHRASE	הנכבד מכל נולד—The most honored of all who are born
HER BLESSING	She will serve to uplift all around her to greater heights. She will be a very special, energetic, and unique human being.

MALKA מלכה

VARIANT	Malkah
HEBREW	A queen
GEMATRIA	95
HER WORD	יפה—Beautiful (Gen. 39:6)
HER PHRASE	טוב וחסד—Goodness and kindness
HER BLESSING	She will be beautiful inside and out. She will always act in a good and just manner.

MANGENA מנגינה

HEBREW	Song, melody
GEMATRIA	158
HER WORD	ונבנים—And understanding (Deut. 1:13)
HER PHRASE	זו נאה וחסודה—This one is beautiful and gracious
HER BLESSING	Wisdom and understanding will be among her greatest attributes. She will be renowned for her beauty and kindness.

MARGANIT מרגנית

HEBREW	A plant in Israel
GEMATRIA	703
HER WORD	מסגרת—A border (Ex. 25:25)
	אוצרות—Treasure, wealth, riches
HER PHRASE	ככתר החן—Like a crown of charm
HER BLESSING	She will know how, when, and where to set limits. She will be a source of treasure and riches to all.

MARGOLIT מרגלית

VARIANT	Margalit
HEBREW	Pearl
GEMATRIA	683
HER WORD	תרגיע—You shall have ease (Deut. 28:65)
HER PHRASE	האשה חשובה מאוד—A very important woman
HER BLESSING	Her life will be one of ease and success. She will accomplish very important things during her lifetime.

MARNINA מרנינה

HEBREW	Causing to sing
GEMATRIA	355
HER WORD	בשמחה—With joy (Gen. 31:27)
HER PHRASE	אדם יקר—A precious person
HER BLESSING	To celebrate life with joy. She will be a most precious gift.

MARTA מרתה

VARIANT	Marsa, Martha
HEBREW	Lady
GEMATRIA	645
HER WORD	השמש—The sun (Gen. 15:12)
HER PHRASE	לבה לב מבין דעת—Her heart is one of profound understanding
HER BLESSING	She will be a ray of sunshine to all around her. She will have an intuitive understanding.

MARVA מרוה

HEBREW	Sage, a plant
GEMATRIA	251
HER WORD	המראה—The appearance
HER PHRASE	כי יבנה ויצליח—Because she will build and succeed
HER BLESSING	Her appearance and her actions will be pleasing to all. She will successfully reach her goals in life.

MASADA מסדה

HEBREW	Foundation
GEMATRIA	109
HER WORD	ומזון—And food (Gen. 45:23)
HER PHRASE	גדל חסד—Greatness of mercy
HER BLESSING	She will be known for her kindness in feeding friends and family. Goodness and charity will always be a part of her life.

MASHA משה

VARIANT	Mashe
HEBREW	Feminine form of Moshe (salvation)
GEMATRIA	345
HER WORD	שמה*—Her name (Gen. 11:9)
HER PHRASE	חיים ארוכים—A long life
HER BLESSING	She will bring honor and glory to her name. She will live a long and illustrious life.

MATANA מתנה

HEBREW	Gift
GEMATRIA	495
HER WORD	תמימה—Without blemish (Lev. 4:28)
HER PHRASE	שלמים בחכמה—Complete with wisdom
HER BLESSING	She will be pure of body and soul. She will be wise to all situations.

MATILDA מתילדה

OLD GERMAN	Strong one
GEMATRIA	489
HER WORD	החלמות—The dreams (Gen. 37:19)
HER PHRASE	שמחה וצהלה—Joy and celebration
HER BLESSING	She will fulfill her dreams and desires. Her life will be joyous and the cause for much celebration.

MATRONA מתרונה

LATIN	An old woman
GEMATRIA	701
HER WORD	והפרתי—And I will make fruitful (Gen. 17:6)
HER PHRASE	חתן מזל טוב כלה מזל טוב—Groom good luck, bride good luck
HER BLESSING	She will bear the fruit of God's blessings. She will enjoy a successful marriage.

MAXIMA מקסימה

HEBREW	Miracle worker, enchanter
GEMATRIA	255
HER WORD	נאדר—Glorious (Ex. 15:11)
HER PHRASE	טובה וברכה—Goodness and blessing
HER BLESSING	Her future will be glorious and bright. Goodness and blessing will be parts of her life.

MAYAN מעיין

HEBREW	Spring fountain
GEMATRIA	180
HER WORD	עינים*—The eyes (Gen. 20:16)
HER PHRASE	מאביך ומאמך—From your father and your mother
HER BLESSING	She will continue the great deeds of her ancestors and serve as a foundation of blessing to her community.

MAZAL מזל

HEBREW	Good luck, a star
GEMATRIA	77
HER WORD	מלאו—Are fulfilled (Gen. 29:21)
HER PHRASE	טוב לב וחביב—A good heart and beloved
HER BLESSING	All her dreams and wishes will be fulfilled. Her good heart will endear her to all.

MECHOLA מחולה

VARIANT	Mehola
HEBREW	Dance
GEMATRIA	89
HER WORD	יעדה—Designated (Ex. 21:8)
HER PHRASE	ולבה לב זהב—And her heart is golden
HER BLESSING	She was designated for greatness. The goodness of her heart will influence all her deeds.

MEIRA מאירה

HEBREW	Enlightening, light
GEMATRIA	256
HER WORD	ומבחר—And the chosen (Ex. 15:4)
HER PHRASE	נכבד מכל נולד—The most honored of all who are born
HER BLESSING	She will be chosen for greatness. She will bring great honor and joy to those in her life.

MENACHEMA מנחמה

HEBREW	Consolation, comforter
GEMATRIA	143
HER WORD	הצליח—Prospered (Gen. 24:56)
HER PHRASE	מלאה כל טוב—Full of only good
HER BLESSING	She will prosper in all that she undertakes. She will be totally infused with goodness, spending much time comforting the afflicted.

MENORA מנורה

HEBREW	A candelabra
GEMATRIA	301
HER WORD	אש—Fire, torch (Gen. 16:17)
HER PHRASE	היא זכורה לטוב—She will be remembered for good
HER BLESSING	She will light the fire of truth and justice. Her reputation for good deeds will both precede her and be remembered afterwards.

MENUCHA מנוחה

HEBREW	Rest
GEMATRIA	109
HER WORD	דיצה—Joy
HER PHRASE	גדל חסד—Great graciousness
HER BLESSING	Her life will be joyous, filled with goodness and graciousness.

METUKA מתוקה

HEBREW	Sweet
GEMATRIA	551
HER WORD	קומה*—Its height (Gen. 6:15)
HER PHRASE	ממנחת אהבה—From the gift of love
HER BLESSING	Her sweet demeanor will bring joy to all. She will reach great heights and she will have abundant love.

MIA מיה

HEBREW	Who is like God
GEMATRIA	55
HER WORD	ימה*—Sea (Ex. 10:19)
HER PHRASE	ידידה טובה—A good friend
HER BLESSING	She will successfully ride the seas of life. Her devotion to friends and family stand out as an example to others.

MICHAELA מיכאלה

HEBREW	Who is like God
GEMATRIA	106
HER WORD	כאל-הים*—Like God (Gen. 3:5)
HER PHRASE	יחיד ומיוחד—One and only
HER BLESSING	She will be pure and godly in her endeavors, and have a very special and unique personality.

MICHAL מיכל

HEBREW	Small stream
GEMATRIA	100
HER WORD	מלכי*—Kings of (Gen. 17:16)
HER PHRASE	לב חכם—Wise heart
HER BLESSING	She will be a leader of mankind. She will be all wise and knowing.

MIGDALA מגדלה

HEBREW	Tower, fortress
GEMATRIA	82
HER WORD	עזה—Strong (Ex. 14:21)
	ניחוח—Sweet, pleasant (Ex. 29:18)
HER PHRASE	כבוד אב ואם—Honoring father and mother
HER BLESSING	She will serve as a source of strength to those around her. She will have a sweet and endearing demeanor. She will exemplify a perfect daughter, bringing honor to her parents.

MIGDANA מגדנה

HEBREW	Gift
GEMATRIA	102
HER WORD	נחמד—Pleasant (Gen. 2:9)
HER PHRASE	בחכם לב—With a wise heart
HER BLESSING	She will be most pleasing. She will join wisdom with compassion.

MILI מילי

HEBREW	Who is for me
GEMATRIA	90
HER WORD	יודע—Shall be known (Gen. 41:31)
HER PHRASE	הלב החם—The warm heart
HER BLESSING	She will enjoy an impeccable reputation. She will be a warm and giving individual.

MINA מינה

VARIANT	Mena
HEBREW	Of a kind
GEMATRIA	105
HER WORD	גבעל—Blossoming (Ex. 9:31)
HER PHRASE	וילדה טובה ואדיבה—A good and well-mannered girl
HER BLESSING	Her plans will always come to successful fruition. Her polite and gentle demeanor will endear her to all.

MIRIAM מרים

HEBREW	Mistress of the sea
GEMATRIA	290
HER WORD	מרים*—Set apart, lift up (Ex. 35:24)
HER PHRASE	ומה רב טובך—And how abundant is your goodness
HER BLESSING	She will be most unique and very special, being able to uplift and elevate others. She will be the epitome of goodness.

MITZPA מצפה

HEBREW	Tower
GEMATRIA	215
HER WORD	זרח—Shone (Gen. 38:30)
HER PHRASE	נס היה פה—A miracle occured here
HER BLESSING	She will shine and beautify all that she is involved in. The miracle of her birth will bring joy to all.

MORASHA מורשה

HEBREW	Inheritance, heritage
GEMATRIA	551
HER WORD	ראשים—Heads (Gen. 2:10)
HER PHRASE	ממנחה אהבה—From the gift of love
HER BLESSING	Her sweet demeanor will bring joy to all. Her heritage will be with the heads and leaders of our people.

MORIA מוריה

HEBREW	Teacher
GEMATRIA	261
HER WORD	וימהר*—And he hurried (Gen. 18:6)
HER PHRASE	עניו מכל אדם—Most modest of people
HER BLESSING	Her gift will be the ability to teach and communicate. She will humbly and hurriedly carry out all of her ambitions.

MORIEL מוריאל

HEBREW	God is my teacher, my guide
GEMATRIA	287
HER WORD	ורפא—And heal (Ex. 21:19)
HER PHRASE	פלא יועץ—A wondrous advisor
HER BLESSING	She will be gifted with unique insight. She will possess the power to heal and teach.

M O R I T מורית

HEBREW	God is my teacher
GEMATRIA	656
HER WORD	התרומה—The priestly offering (Ex. 25:3)
HER PHRASE	וכחבה יתרה—And like extra love
HER BLESSING	She will deal with all in a forthright and righteous manner. She will be exceptionally loving and giving to all.

N

NAAMAH נעמה

HEBREW	Pleasant, beautiful
GEMATRIA	165
HER WORD	הכסף—The silver (Gen. 23:16)
HER PHRASE	לחיים טובים—To a good life
HER BLESSING	Her pleasant and charming demeanor will bring joy to all. Her success and her wealth will insure her and those around her a good life.

NAAMI נעמי

VARIANT	Naomi
HEBREW	Pleasant
GEMATRIA	170
HER WORD	לעלם—Forever (Gen. 3:22)
HER PHRASE	קול אוהבך—The voice of your beloved
HER BLESSING	Her love will be eternal. The sound of love will forever surround her.

NAARA נערה

HEBREW	Girl, young woman
GEMATRIA	325
HER WORD	ויגשו—And they drew near (Gen. 19:9)
HER PHRASE	הפנים לעם—Face to the people
HER BLESSING	From youth, she will be communal-minded, drawing near to others and helping people.

NACHALAH נחלה

HEBREW	Inherited, inheritance, brook
GEMATRIA	93
HER WORD	ידעי—Knowing (Gen. 3:5)
HER PHRASE	באהבה וחסד—With love and kindness
HER BLESSING	She will be wise and all-knowing. Her loving kindness will impact all that she does.

NAGIDA נגידה

HEBREW	Wealthy, prosperous ruler
GEMATRIA	72
HER WORD	חסד—Kindness, goodness (Gen. 24:12)
HER PHRASE	היא נאה—She is beautiful
HER BLESSING	Her kindness will permeate all that she does. She will be beautiful both within and without.

NAMIT נעמית

HEBREW	Ostrich-like bird
GEMATRIA	570
HER WORD	מעינת*—Fountains (Gen. 8:2)
HER PHRASE	יושר לבבך—Your righteous heart
HER BLESSING	She will be a wellspring of joy and happiness. She will bring true fulfillment and joy to all those around her.

NANA נענע

VARIANT	Naana
HEBREW	Mint
GEMATRIA	240
HER WORD	פעמים—Twice (Gen. 27:36)
HER PHRASE	וברכה בה—And blessing in her
HER BLESSING	She will be doubly blessed. She will be a source of blessing to all.

NASIA נסיה

HEBREW	Miracle of God
GEMATRIA	125
HER WORD	החזקה—The strong (Deut. 3:24)
HER PHRASE	ייטב לבבכם—Will gladden your hearts
HER BLESSING	She will be strong of spirit and character. She will bring joy to all who know her.

NATANIA נתניה

HEBREW	Gift of God
GEMATRIA	515
HER WORD	ואתחנן—And I prayed (Deut. 3:23)
HER PHRASE	נגילה ונשמחה בו—Be happy and rejoice therein
HER BLESSING	She will be the answer to all your prayers. She will be a constant source of happiness and joy.

NAVA נאוה

HEBREW	Beautiful
GEMATRIA	62
HER WORD	לכבוד—For splendor (Ex. 28:2)
HER PHRASE	טוב מאד—Very good
HER BLESSING	She will bring honor and glory to your name. Her goodness will be evident in all that she does.

NECHAMA נחמה

VARIANT	Nehama
HEBREW	A comfort
GEMATRIA	103
HER WORD	מנחה*—Present (Gen. 4:3)
HER PHRASE	לכבוד אם—To the honor of mother
HER BLESSING	She will be a most cherished gift from on High. She will bring honor and glory to her entire family.

NEDIVA נדיבה

HEBREW	Noble, generous
GEMATRIA	71
HER WORD	מא-ל—From God (Gen. 49:25)
HER PHRASE	מדה טובה—Good character
HER BLESSING	She is a gift from on High. Her character and deportment will be above reproach.

NEGINA נגינה

HEBREW	Song, melody
GEMATRIA	118
HER WORD	חכמים—Wise (Deut. 1:13)
HER PHRASE	טוב ויפה—Good and beautiful
HER BLESSING	She will be all-knowing and beautiful both within and without.

NEORA נאורה

HEBREW	Light
GEMATRIA	262
HER WORD	ונראה*—And we shall see (Gen. 37:20)
HER PHRASE	בברכה כזו—With a blessing like this
HER BLESSING	She will be a source of enlightenment. She will have an abundance of blessings and success.

NESHAMA נשמה

HEBREW	Soul, spirit
GEMATRIA	395
HER WORD	השמים—The heavens (Gen. 1:1)
HER PHRASE	כאשה הגונה—Like a proper woman
HER BLESSING	Blessed with a spiritual nature, she will enjoy etheral qualities and serve others as a role model.

NETA נטע

HEBREW	A plant
GEMATRIA	129
HER WORD	ערנה—Pleasure (Gen. 18:12)
HER PHRASE	לילדה טובה ואריבה—To a polite, good girl
HER BLESSING	She will bring great pleasure to all. Her well-mannered demeanor is one of her most endearing qualities.

NILI נילי

HEBREW	"Israel's triumph shall not fail" (An acronym of the Hebrew words נצח ישראל לא ישקר from Sam. I 15:29)
GEMATRIA	100
HER WORD	מלכי—Kings of (Gen. 17:16)
HER PHRASE	לב חכם—Wise heart
HER BLESSING	She will be a leader of mankind. She will be wise and all-knowing.

NIMA נימה

VARIANT	Nema
HEBREW	A thread, a hair
GEMATRIA	105
HER WORD	גבעל—Blossoming (Ex. 9:31)
HER PHRASE	וילדה טובה ואריבה—A good and well-mannered girl
HER BLESSING	Her plans will always come to successful fruition. Her polite and gentle demeanor will endear her to all.

NIRA נירה

HEBREW	Beam or loom, uncultivated field
GEMATRIA	265
HER WORD	נאדרי—Glorious (Ex. 15:6)
HER PHRASE	פעמים באהבה—Two times with love
HER BLESSING	Her future will take her along a glorious path. She will be most beloved and doubly blessed.

NIRIT נירית

HEBREW	A flowering plant in Israel
GEMATRIA	670
HER WORD	שלשם—Day before yesterday (Gen. 31:5)
HER PHRASE	גם בחיים של ברכה—Also with a life of blessing
HER BLESSING	Her past will be the foundation upon which she will build a successful future. Her life will be full of blessings, and she will be a source of joy to those around her.

NISA נסה

HEBREW	Sign, emblem
GEMATRIA	115
HER WORD	חזק—Steadfast, strong (Gen. 41:57)
HER PHRASE	אהבה ללא גבול—Love without an end
HER BLESSING	Strong and steadfast, she will be a source of wisdom endowed with endless love.

NITZA נצה

HEBREW	Flower bud
GEMATRIA	145
HER WORD	מטמון—Treasure (Gen. 43:23)
HER PHRASE	טובך וחסידך—Your goodness and your kindness
HER BLESSING	She will be a treasure to all. She will be acknowledged as a source of goodness and kindness.

NITZANA ניצנה

HEBREW	Flower bud
GEMATRIA	205
HER WORD	וצדקה—And righteousness (Deut. 6:25)
HER PHRASE	קול האוהבים—The voice of those who love
	היודע ללמוד—One who has the wisdom to learn
HER BLESSING	Righteousness will be her way of life with the sound of love always surrounding her. She will be a wonderful student.

NOFIA נופיה

HEBREW	God's beautiful panoramic landscape
GEMATRIA	151
HER WORD	ומעלה—And upward (Lev. 27:7)
HER PHRASE	קול חבה—The sound of love
HER BLESSING	Her sights will always be set high and she will achieve her goals. She will be a voice for love and devotion.

NOGA נוגה

HEBREW	Shining, morning light
GEMATRIA	64
HER WORD	מידי—By the hands (Gen. 49:24)
HER PHRASE	ידיד הא-ל—Beloved by God
HER BLESSING	She will be a vehicle for bringing goodness to mankind. She will be blessed with joy and good fortune.

NOYA נויה

HEBREW	Beautiful, ornamental
GEMATRIA	71
HER WORD	מלא—Full (Gen. 23:9)
HER PHRASE	ידה בכל—Her hand is in everything
HER BLESSING	She will always be busy with many projects and find fulfillment in her beautiful accomplishments.

NOYVA נויוה

VARIANT	Nova
HEBREW	Bejewelled, adorned by nature
GEMATRIA	77
HER WORD	מלאו—Are fulfilled (Gen. 29:21)
HER PHRASE	טוב לב וחביב—A good heart and beloved
HER BLESSING	All her dreams and wishes will be fulfilled. Her good heart will endear her to all.

NUCHA נוחה

HEBREW	Restful
GEMATRIA	69
HER WORD	וכלביא—And as a lioness (Gen. 49:9)
HER PHRASE	לאהבה ואחוה—For love and fellowship
HER BLESSING	She will be both a leader and protector of her family, as a lioness. The essence of her being will be devoted to love.

NURIT נורית

HEBREW	Light
GEMATRIA	666
HER WORD	ויתרן*—And their excess (Gen. 36:26)
HER PHRASE	אז ברכה תהיי—Then may you be blessed
	כל התורה—The entire Torah
HER BLESSING	She will be showered with an excess of blessings. Her life will fulfill all the ideals of the Torah.

O

ODEDA עודדה

HEBREW	Strong, courageous
GEMATRIA	89
HER WORD	החלום—The dream (Gen. 37:6)
	יעדה—Designated her (Ex. 21:8)
HER PHRASE	ולבה לב זהב—And her heart will be golden
HER BLESSING	Her life will be a dream. She will have a pure and generous heart and has been destined for greatness.

ODEHLIYA אודהליה

HEBREW	I will praise God
GEMATRIA	61
HER WORD	מיטב—From the best (Ex. 22:4)
HER PHRASE	ילד טוב—A good child
HER BLESSING	To be always full of joy and goodness. She will be an ideal child.

OFRAH אפרה

VARIANT	Oprah
HEBREW	Dust
GEMATRIA	286
HER WORD	פרו—Be fruitful (Gen. 1:22)
HER PHRASE	חבר נכבד—Honored friend
HER BLESSING	She will be fruitful and multiply. She will make a most devoted and special friend.

OPHIRA עפירה

HEBREW	Lead
GEMATRIA	365
HER WORD	השכם—Rise up early (Ex. 8:16)
HER PHRASE	ברצון טוב—With good will, agreeably
HER BLESSING	She will be quick to do good, and she will reach profound depths in her understanding.

ORA אורה

HEBREW	Light
GEMATRIA	212
HER WORD	ירב—Will multiply (Gen. 1:22)
HER PHRASE	עם חיים בכבוד—With a life of honor
HER BLESSING	She will be fruitful and multiply. She will live her life in an honorable manner.

ORAHLEE אורהלי

HEBREW	Light, light is mine
GEMATRIA	252
HER WORD	לברך—To bless (Gen. 27:30)
HER PHRASE	לב טהור—A pure heart
HER BLESSING	She will always be a source of joy and blessing. She will be pure of heart and soul.

ORLEE אורלי

HEBREW	Light, light is mine
GEMATRIA	247
HER WORD	יאריכו—They will be lengthened (Deut. 25:15)
HER PHRASE	לב הדור—The heart of the generation
HER BLESSING	Her life will be one of song and cheer as well as long duration. She will be the heart and soul of her people.

ORNA ארנה

VARIANT	Arna
HEBREW	Pine tree or "Let there be light"
GEMATRIA	256
HER WORD	ומבחר—And the chosen (Ex. 15:4)
HER PHRASE	נכבד מכל נולד—The most honored of all who are born
HER BLESSING	She will be chosen for greatness. She will bring great honor and joy to those around her.

ORPAH ערפה

HEBREW	Fawn
GEMATRIA	355
HER WORD	בשמחה—Joy (Gen. 31:27)
HER PHRASE	אדם יקר—A precious person
HER BLESSING	She will celebrate life with joy. She will be a most precious gift.

P

PAZ פז

HEBREW	Gold
GEMATRIA	87
HER WORD	ויהללו—And they praised (Gen. 12:15)
HER PHRASE	אחד מיוחד—One and only
HER BLESSING	All who know and love her will sing her praises. She will be unique and precious as gold.

PAZIA פזיה

HEBREW	Gold of God
GEMATRIA	102
HER WORD	נחמד—Pleasant (Gen. 2:9)
HER PHRASE	בחכם לב—With a wise heart
HER BLESSING	She will be most pleasing. She will join wisdom with compassion.

PENINA פנינה

VARIANT	Peninah
HEBREW	Coral or pearl
GEMATRIA	195
HER WORD	הפסים—Colors (Gen. 37:23)
HER PHRASE	ילדה יחידה במינה—A girl who is one of a kind
HER BLESSING	She will have a colorful personality. She will be unique and special in every way.

PERACHYA פרחיה

HEBREW	Flowerful
GEMATRIA	303
HER WORD	שזרעך—And your seed (Gen. 17:9)
HER PHRASE	ילד נהדר—An outstanding child
HER BLESSING	She and her descendants will be special. She will be a gracious, unique child.

PERI פרי

HEBREW	Fruit
GEMATRIA	290
HER WORD	רץ—Ran (Gen. 18:7)
HER PHRASE	ל"ו צדיקים—The 36 righteous people
HER BLESSING	In her merit, others will be fruitful and prosper.

PIYUTA פיוטה

HEBREW	Poet, poetry
GEMATRIA	110
HER WORD	כמים—Like water (Gen. 49:4)
HER PHRASE	כטוב המיוחד—As uniquely good
HER BLESSING	She will add poetry and beauty to the world. Her goodness and unique personality will bring much joy to all.

PORIYAH פוריה

HEBREW	Fruitful
GEMATRIA	301
HER WORD	אש—Fire, torch (Gen. 16:17)
HER PHRASE	היא זכורה לטוב—She will be remembered for good
HER BLESSING	She will light the fire of truth and justice. Her reputation for good deeds will both precede her and be remembered afterwards.

PRIVA פריוה

HEBREW	Fruitful
GEMATRIA	301
HER WORD	אש—Fire, torch (Gen. 16:17)
HER PHRASE	היא זכורה לטוב—She will be remembered for good
HER BLESSING	She will light the fire of truth and justice. Her reputation for good deeds will both precede her and be remembered afterwards.

PUAH פועה

HEBREW	To cry aloud
GEMATRIA	161
HER WORD	ונעלה—And go up to (Gen. 35:3)
HER PHRASE	מזל חיינו—The luck of one's lives
HER BLESSING	She will ascend to great heights. She will be a source of good luck to all.

R

RACHAMA רחמה

HEBREW	Young woman
GEMATRIA	253
HER WORD	להריח—To give off a pleasant odor (Ex. 30:38)
HER PHRASE	בדרך הטובה—In the correct way
HER BLESSING	Her good name will spread like perfume. She will always walk in the righteous path.

RACHEL רחל

HEBREW	Ewe, sheep
GEMATRIA	238
HER WORD	ויברך—And he blessed (Gen. 1:22)
HER PHRASE	ויהי אור—And there was light
HER BLESSING	She will be a source of great wealth both materially and spiritually. She will bring light and wisdom to others.

RAMA רמה

HEBREW	Lofty, exalted
GEMATRIA	245
HER WORD	וברזל—And iron (Gen. 4:22)
HER PHRASE	ונמצא חן—And she will find favor
HER BLESSING	She will be strong and determined. She will find favor in the eyes of all.

RANANA רעננה

HEBREW	Fresh
GEMATRIA	375
HER WORD	שלמה—Perfect (Deut. 25:15)
HER PHRASE	מורה ומחנך—A teacher and an educator
HER BLESSING	She will be perfect both outwardly and inwardly. She will set an example to others.

RANI רני

HEBREW	She is singing
GEMATRIA	260
HER WORD	ירים—Lift up (Gen. 41:44)
HER PHRASE	גמר טוב—A good conclusion (sealing)
HER BLESSING	With song and laughter, she will lift the spirit of others and ensure happy endings.

RAPHAELA רפאלה

HEBREW	God has healed
GEMATRIA	316
HER WORD	ויפרך—And make you fruitful (Gen. 28:3)
HER PHRASE	הקול הנעים—The pleasant voice
HER BLESSING	She will have many descendants. She will bring much music and joy into the lives of those around her.

RAVITAL רויטל

HEBREW	God is my provider (of dew)
GEMATRIA	255
HER WORD	נאדר—Glorious (Ex. 15:11)
HER PHRASE	טובה וברכה—Goodness and blessing
HER BLESSING	Her future will be glorious and bright. Goodness and blessing will enrich her life.

RAYA רעיה

HEBREW	Female friend
GEMATRIA	285
HER WORD	העיר*—The city (Gen. 4:17)
HER PHRASE	רוח נדיבה—A giving spirit
HER BLESSING	A friend to all, she will be known for her generous spirit and compassionate nature.

RAZILEE רזילי

ARAMAIC AND HEBREW	My secret
GEMATRIA	257
HER WORD	לזכר—To remember (Gen. 9:16)
HER PHRASE	בטובה וברכה—With goodness and blessing
HER BLESSING	She will be a most memorable person. All that she does will be a source of blessing and joy.

RE'UT רעות

HEBREW	Friendship, companionship
GEMATRIA	676
HER WORD	ותער*—And she emptied (Gen. 24:20)
HER PHRASE	הזן את העולם כולו—Feeds the whole world
HER BLESSING	She will empty her own pockets, in complete friendship, to help sustain others.

RICKMA רקמה

HEBREW	A woven product
GEMATRIA	345
HER WORD	שמה—Her name (Gen. 11:9)
HER PHRASE	חיים ארוכים—A long life
HER BLESSING	She will bring honor and glory to her name. She will live a long and illustrious life.

RIMONA רמונה

HEBREW	A pomegranate
GEMATRIA	301
HER WORD	אש—Fire, torch (Gen. 16:17)
HER PHRASE	היא זכורה לטוב—She will be remembered for her goodness
HER BLESSING	She will light the fire of truth and justice. Her reputation for good deeds will both precede her and be remembered afterwards.

RINA רינה

VARIANT	Rena
HEBREW	Joy, song
GEMATRIA	265
HER WORD	נאדרי—Glorious (Ex. 15:6)
HER PHRASE	נבונה ונאמנה—Understanding and faithful
HER BLESSING	She will bring joy and song to all who know her. She will have deep understanding and be extremely dependable.

RIVA ריבה

HEBREW	Maiden
GEMATRIA	217
HER WORD	ירבה*—Will increase (Ex. 30:15)
HER PHRASE	לך מחיל אל חיל—Go from strength to strength
HER BLESSING	She will evermore increase her abilities, her strengths, and her blessings, and she will grow from strength to strength.

RIVKA רבקה

VARIANT	Rivkah
HEBREW	Bound, to tie, to bind
GEMATRIA	307
HER WORD	הבקר*—The morning (Gen. 44:3)
HER PHRASE	רוח אל-הים בה—The spirit of God is in her
HER BLESSING	She will possess the brightness and joy of morning. The spirit of God will dwell in her.

ROMIA רומיה

HEBREW	Height, lofty
GEMATRIA	261
HER WORD	הדברים—The words (Gen. 15:1)
	מוריה*—The name of the mountain designated for the sacrifice of Isaac as well as the holy temple
HER PHRASE	ענו מכל אדם—The most humble of all mankind
HER BLESSING	Humility, sacrifice, and spirituality will be her characteristics. Her words will serve to elevate the thoughts and deeds of others.

RONIT רונית

HEBREW	Song
GEMATRIA	666
HER WORD	ויתרן*—And an excess (Gen. 36:26)
HER PHRASE	אז ברכה תהיי כל התורה—The entire Torah will be her blessing
HER BLESSING	She will be surrounded by blessing. Her life will fulfill all the ideals of the Torah.

RUTH רות

HEBREW	Friendship
GEMATRIA	606
HER WORD	תדבר—You will speak (Gen. 31:24)
HER PHRASE	בח צחוק—A smile
HER BLESSING	With a smile on her lips, she will speak words of friendship that will endear her to many.

S

SAGIT שׂגית

HEBREW	Sublime, lofty
GEMATRIA	713
HER WORD	ואשתו—And his wife (Gen. 2:25)
HER PHRASE	בריאות הגוף—Health of body
HER BLESSING	Sound of mind and healthy in body, she will enjoy a very happy marriage and be blessed with excellent family life.

SARA שׂרה

HEBREW	Noble, princess
GEMATRIA	505
HER WORD	נתנה—She gave (Gen. 5:12)
HER PHRASE	וילכו שניהם יחדו—And the two of them walked together
HER BLESSING	With noble, princely bearing she will make an outstanding friend and partner.

SARIT שׂרית

HEBREW	Noble, princess
GEMATRIA	910
HER WORD	יירש*—Who possesses (Num. 36:8)
HER PHRASE	ברכות לרבים—Blessings to many
HER BLESSING	She will be blessed with princely possessions that she will use as a source of blessing to others.

SHACHAR שחר

HEBREW	Dawn
GEMATRIA	508
HER WORD	חרש*—An engraver (Ex. 28:11)
HER PHRASE	שמחה נעלה—Hidden joy
HER BLESSING	She will engrave a lasting impression on others. As the dawn brings in its wake much warmth and light, so will she reveal her inner joy to others.

SHALVA שלוה

VARIANT	Shalvah
HEBREW	Calmness, tranquility
GEMATRIA	341
HER WORD	לארצך—To your land (Gen. 32:10)
HER PHRASE	עמוד הגבורה—Pillar of strength
HER BLESSING	She will be a pillar of strength and tranquility, firmly committed to her family, her land, and her people.

SHARON שרון

HEBREW	Plain, flat area
GEMATRIA	556
HER WORD	הראשון—The first (Ex. 12:15)
HER PHRASE	לאהבת חכמים—To the love of the wise
HER BLESSING	She will be a leader and first among her peers. She will be drawn to knowledge and will find a mentor to guide her.

SHEBA שבע

HEBREW	Oath
GEMATRIA	372
HER WORD	עשב*—Herb, grass (Gen. 1:11)
HER PHRASE	רב ניסים—Many miracles
HER BLESSING	She will be especially fruitful. Her word will be her bond and her life will be blessed with miraculous occurences.

SHIFRA שִׁיפְרָה

HEBREW	Good, beautiful
GEMATRIA	595
HER WORD	מנקתה—Her nurse (Gen. 24:59)
HER PHRASE	ראה ברכה בעמלך—See blessing from your toil
HER BLESSING	She will work diligently and experience much joy from her labor. She will be known for her goodness and beauty.

SHIMRA שִׁמְרָה

HEBREW	Guarded, protected
GEMATRIA	545
HER WORD	*השמר—The keeper (Gen. 4:9)
HER PHRASE	לב רגיש—A sensitive heart
HER BLESSING	She will guard whatever is entrusted to her with feeling and compassion.

SHIRA שִׁירָה

HEBREW	Song
GEMATRIA	515
HER WORD	*ירשה—A possession (Num. 24:18)
HER PHRASE	אין בך שום מום—There is in you no defect
HER BLESSING	A perfect treasure who inspires song in all those who know her.

SHLOMIT שְׁלוּמִית

HEBREW	Peace, peaceful
GEMATRIA	786
HER WORD	ועשית—And you shall do (Gen. 40:14)
HER PHRASE	שם ותהלה—A name and praise
HER BLESSING	She will do much and achieve fame and praise. Her peaceful ways will bring much blessing.

SHLOM-TZIYON שלום-ציון

HEBREW	Peace of Zion
GEMATRIA	532
HER WORD	ורכשו—And his wealth (Gen. 14:16)
HER PHRASE	הדור החדש—The new generation
HER BLESSING	She will creatively display the benefits of the new generation who will bring peace to Zion.

SHOSHANA שושנה

HEBREW	A rose, a lily
GEMATRIA	661
HER WORD	הנרות—The candles (Lev. 24:4)
HER PHRASE	מהורים יקרים—From precious parentage
HER BLESSING	She will be a beacon of light to her noble ancestors.

SHULA שולה

HEBREW	Peace, peaceful
GEMATRIA	341
HER WORD	השלו*—The quail (Ex. 16:13)
HER PHRASE	סוד הצמצום—The secret of self-containment, concealment
HER BLESSING	She will bring about peace between others by virtue of her modesty and self-effacement.

SHULAMIT שולמית

HEBREW	Peaceful
GEMATRIA	786
HER WORD	וספרתם—And you shall count (Lev. 23:15)
HER PHRASE	המחשבה והמעשה—The thought and the deed
HER BLESSING	Both her thoughts and her actions will be recounted as exemplars of peace.

SIGAL סיגל

HEBREW	Color violet, flower
GEMATRIA	103
HER WORD	הכוכבים—The stars (Gen. 1:16)
HER PHRASE	לך הגדולה—To you is greatness
HER BLESSING	She will be looked up to, as the stars in the heavens, and continue to grow and flourish.

SIMA סימה

ARAMAIC	A treasure
GEMATRIA	115
HER WORD	חזק—Steadfast (Gen. 41:57)
HER PHRASE	כבוד ועז—Honor and strength
HER BLESSING	She will be treasured for her constancy and will find honor and glory.

SIMCHA שמחה

HEBREW	Joy
GEMATRIA	353
HER WORD	חמשה*—Five (Gen. 18:28)
HER PHRASE	אהבה שם—Love is there
HER BLESSING	With joy, she delights in the teachings of the five books of the Torah and treasures love above all.

SMADAR סמדר

HEBREW	Bud, blossom
GEMATRIA	304
HER WORD	בבקר—In the morning (Gen. 19:27)
HER PHRASE	הצלחה נפלאה—Astounding success
HER BLESSING	She will blossom and mature at a very early age and achieve great success.

SOVEL סובל

VARIANT	Sobel
HEBREW	Sustaining
GEMATRIA	98
HER WORD	כוכבים—Stars (Gen. 37:9)
HER PHRASE	כוכב הגאולה—The star of redemption
HER BLESSING	She will sustain her loved ones and redeem them as the stars shine above.

T

TAGA תגה

ARABIC AND ARAMAIC	A crown
GEMATRIA	408
HER WORD	אהבת—You love (Gen. 22:2)
HER PHRASE	כי מה' יצא הדבר—For from the Almighty has the thing been decreed
	(ה' refers to God's four letter name equaling 26)
HER BLESSING	Love and royalty are her gifts as proclaimed from the heavens above.

TALI טלי

VARIANTS	Talya, Teli
HEBREW	My dew
GEMATRIA	49
HER WORD	ואגדלה—And I will make great (Gen. 12:2)
HER PHRASE	לב טוב—A good heart
HER BLESSING	She will find greatness as a reward for her goodness.

TALMA תלמה

HEBREW	Mound, hill
GEMATRIA	475
HER WORD	עתה—Now (Gen. 19:9)
HER PHRASE	מורה דרך—One who leads the way
HER BLESSING	She will always seize the right moment and lead others to the top of the mountain.

TALMOR תלמור

HEBREW	Heaped or sprinkled with myrrh (spice), perfumed
GEMATRIA	676
HER WORD	ולשמש—And to the sun (Deut. 17:3)
HER PHRASE	בירושלים הבנויה—In rebuilt Jerusalem
HER BLESSING	She will be sprinkled with the beauty of the sun and the glory of Jerusalem restored.

TALOR טלאור

HEBREW	Dew of the morning
GEMATRIA	246
HER WORD	להאיר—To give light (Gen. 1:15)
HER PHRASE	כל חיי העולם הזה—All of life of this world
HER BLESSING	She will enjoy this world to the fullest, every day bringing the light and the dew of renewed blessing.

TAMAR תמר

VARIANT	Tamara
HEBREW	A palm tree
GEMATRIA	640
HER WORD	שמש—The sun (Deut. 4:41)
HER PHRASE	זאת הברכה—This is the blessing
HER BLESSING	She will be an independent source of light and blessing.

TECHIYA תחיה

HEBREW	Rebirth, resurrection
GEMATRIA	423
HER WORD	ותגיד—And tell (Ex. 19:3)
HER PHRASE	אות היא—She is a sign
HER BLESSING	She will teach others and be a sign unto them by her deeds. She will bring new life and new meaning to her friends and family.

TEHILLAH תהילה

HEBREW	Praise
GEMATRIA	450
HER WORD	תן—Give (Gen. 14:21)
HER PHRASE	דור לדור—From generation to generation
HER BLESSING	She will have a giving nature linking her to generations past and future.

TEMIMA תמימה

HEBREW	Whole, honest
GEMATRIA	495
HER WORD	מתנה—A gift (Num. 18:6)
HER PHRASE	כי ברך אברכך—For I shall surely bless you
HER BLESSING	She will be a special gift from God and will be doubly blessed.

TEMIRA תמירה

HEBREW	Tall
GEMATRIA	655
HER WORD	הנרת—The lamps (Ex. 30:7)
HER PHRASE	אשר אין בה מום—Who has no defect
HER BLESSING	She is faultless and, like the lamps of the menorah, serves to illuminate and inspire others.

TERUMA תרומה

HEBREW	An offering, a gift
GEMATRIA	651
HER WORD	ותמהר*—And she hastened (Gen. 24:18)
HER PHRASE	עיון תפילה—Insight into prayer
HER BLESSING	She will be known for her devotion in prayer and her speed to fulfill good deeds.

TESHURA תשורה

HEBREW	A gift
GEMATRIA	911
HER WORD	ראשית—The choicest (Gen. 10:10)
HER PHRASE	חיים שלוים ושאננים—A calm and peaceful life
HER BLESSING	She will be unique. The choicest divine gift, whose peaceful years will demonstrate the Almighty's love.

TIKVAH תקוה

HEBREW	Hope
GEMATRIA	511
HER WORD	ראשי—Heads of (Gen. 3:5)
HER PHRASE	הוד מלכות—The glory of kingship
HER BLESSING	She will be optimistic, intelligent, and regal.

TIMORA תמורה

HEBREW	Tall (like the palm tree)
GEMATRIA	651
HER WORD	תרומה*—A gift (Ex. 25:2)
HER PHRASE	האמת והצדק—Truth and righteousness
HER BLESSING	She will have the gifts of truthfulness and righteousness that will make her stand out among her peers.

TIRA טירה

HEBREW	Encampment, enclosure
GEMATRIA	224
HER WORD	הטהורה—The pure (Gen. 8:20)
HER PHRASE	אחד מני אלף—One out of a thousand
HER BLESSING	She will be recognized as being unique amongst the many for her purity and holiness.

TIRTZA תרצה

HEBREW	Acceptance, willing
GEMATRIA	695
HER WORD	מהרתן—Hurried (Ex. 2:18)
	רצתה*—She desired
HER PHRASE	השלחן ערוך—The set table
HER BLESSING	She will be an agreeable, accommodating person whose table will always be set for hospitality.

TIRZAH תרזה

HEBREW	Cypress tree
GEMATRIA	612
HER WORD	ברית—Covenant (Gen. 9:13)
HER PHRASE	ה' רועי לא אחסר—The Lord is my shepherd, I shall not want (ה refers to God's four letter name equaling 26)
HER BLESSING	Lofty and regal, she will have all that she requires because of her special covenant with God.

TIVONA טבעונה

HEBREW	A lover of nature
GEMATRIA	142
HER WORD	בעיני—In the eyes of (Gen. 6:8)
HER PHRASE	קל מהולל—God is praised
HER BLESSING	She will always see the world with eyes of appreciation for God's gifts of beauty and she will be quick to praise what she beholds.

TOVAH טובה

VARIANT	Tova
HEBREW	Good
GEMATRIA	22
HER WORD	ובזהב—And with gold (Gen. 13:2)
HER PHRASE	ואב אחד—And one father
HER BLESSING	She will personify goodness. Her golden example will demonstrate the beauty of a life dedicated to serve our one Father in Heaven.

TZILLA צילה

VARIANT	Zilah
HEBREW	Protection
GEMATRIA	135
HER WORD	הקל—The voice (Gen. 27:22)
HER PHRASE	אם לנבואה—Mother for prophecy
HER BLESSING	She will possess almost prophetic power to protect others with the wisdom of her voice.

TZIPPORAH צפורה

HEBREW	Bird
GEMATRIA	381
HER WORD	השלום—The peace (Gen. 29:6)
HER PHRASE	משבט יהודה—From the tribe of Judah
HER BLESSING	She will spread her wings with the message of peace in the royal spirit of Judah.

TZIVYAH צביה

HEBREW	Female deer, hind
GEMATRIA	107
HER WORD	נבנה—We will build (Gen. 11:4)
HER PHRASE	מגן דוד—Shield of David
HER BLESSING	She will be a builder and a protector of her family and, with the speed of a deer, will accomplish all she desires.

TZIYONA ציונה

HEBREW	Zion, excellent
GEMATRIA	161
HER WORD	הדבקים—Those who are attached (Deut. 4:4)
HER PHRASE	קול חיבה—The voice of love
HER BLESSING	She will draw others to her with her loving words and excellent demeanor.

TZOPHIYAH צופיה

HEBREW	Looking towards, scout, guard of God
GEMATRIA	191
HER WORD	ופניהם—And their faces (Gen. 9:23)
HER PHRASE	אכן מזל גדול—Indeed great good fortune
HER BLESSING	She will look towards others and bring them the *mazal* she herself enjoys in great measure.

U

URIELA אוריאלה

HEBREW	Light of God
GEMATRIA	253
HER WORD	להריח—To perfume
HER PHRASE	בקול העם—With the voice of the people
HER BLESSING	She will be a spokesperson for others and help to alter the mood and spiritual climate of her community.

URIT אורית

HEBREW	Light, fire
GEMATRIA	617
HER WORD	ויראת*—And you shall revere (Lev. 19:14)
HER PHRASE	היא רצה למצוה קלה—She runs to perform even the smallest mitzvah.
HER BLESSING	She will serve God with passion and punctiliousness, serving as a beacon of light to others.

V

VARDA ורדה

VARIANT	Vardia
HEBREW	Rose
GEMATRIA	215
HER WORD	ההרה—To the mountain (Gen. 12:8)
HER PHRASE	אנחנו מודים—We give thanks
HER BLESSING	Like a rose on the mountaintop, she will inspire us to give thanks to God for her beauty.

VERED ורד

HEBREW	Rose
GEMATRIA	210
HER WORD	לעינים—To the eyes (Gen. 3:6)
HER PHRASE	כל פה לך יודה—All mouths will acknowledge you
HER BLESSING	She will be recognized and acknowledged by everyone for her beauty.

Y

YACOBA יעקבה

VARIANT	Yacova
HEBREW	Supplanter, protector
GEMATRIA	187
HER WORD	זקניך—Your elders (Deut. 21:2)
HER PHRASE	חיי העולם הבא—The life of the world to come
HER BLESSING	She will protect and respect her elders, thereby acquiring a special place in the world to come.

YAEL יעל

VARIANT	Jael
HEBREW	Mountain goat
GEMATRIA ·	110
HER WORD	עלי*—On me (Gen. 20:9)
HER PHRASE	טוב לכל אחד—Good to everyone
HER BLESSING	She will jump like a mountain goat to bring the benefit of her words to everyone she knows.

YAFFAH יפה

VARIANT	Yaffa
HEBREW	Beautiful
GEMATRIA	95
HER WORD	פיה*—Her mouth (Gen. 4:11)
HER PHRASE	יחס טוב—Good inheritance
HER BLESSING	The beauty of her words are the blessings of her ancestry

YAKIRA יקירה

HEBREW	Valuable, precious
GEMATRIA	325
HER WORD	נערה—The young maiden (Gen. 34:3)
HER PHRASE	שעולם קטן—Like a small world
HER BLESSING	Even in youth, she will possess special maturity, as precious in her way as a miniature universe.

YARDENAH ירדנה

VARIANT	Jordana
HEBREW	To descend, flow down
GEMATRIA	269
HER WORD	ואברכם—And I will bless them (Gen. 48:9)
HER PHRASE	עם נס גלוי—With open miracle
HER BLESSING	With quick movements, she will flow forward constantly, demonstrating God's blessings and miracles.

YARKANAH ירקונה

HEBREW	Name of a bird, chloris. Feminine form of green
GEMATRIA	371
HER WORD	נשיאי—The chiefs, the princes of (Ex. 16:22)
HER PHRASE	אהל רחל אמנו—The tent of our mother Rachel
HER BLESSING	Like Rachel of old, she will be a chief of her peers, soaring like a bird to ever greater heights.

YATVA יטבה

HEBREW	Good
GEMATRIA	26
HER WORD	הי—The four letter name for God equaling 26 (Gen. 2:4)
HER PHRASE	זה זהב—This is gold
HER BLESSING	She will be Godly, good, and golden.

YECHIELAH יחיאלה

VARIANT	Yechiela
HEBREW	May God live
GEMATRIA	64
HER WORD	ידים—Hands (Gen. 34:21)
HER PHRASE	די לך—It is sufficient for you
HER BLESSING	Her hands will be sufficient to accomplish all she must do to make God live in her life.

YEDIDAH ידידה

VARIANT	Yedida
HEBREW	Friend, beloved
GEMATRIA	33
HER WORD	כחה—Her strength (Gen. 4:12)
HER PHRASE	באגוד טוב—In good gatherings
HER BLESSING	Her strength will be friendship. She will always find a place of special love in any gathering.

YEHUDIS יהודית

VARIANT	Yehudit
HEBREW	Praised
GEMATRIA	435
HER WORD	הנפש—The soul (Gen. 12:5)
HER PHRASE	חנון ורחום אני—I am gracious and merciful
HER BLESSING	She will be praised for the beauty of her soul and the graciousness of her spirit.

YEIRA יאירה

HEBREW	Light
GEMATRIA	226
HER WORD	ויבחר—And he chose (Gen. 13:11)
HER PHRASE	קול מלך—The voice of a king
HER BLESSING	She will be chosen as a light to others because of the regal quality of her voice.

YEMIMAH ימימה

VARIANT	Yemima
HEBREW	Dove
GEMATRIA	105
HER WORD	לכהן—To serve spiritually (Ex. 29:1)
HER PHRASE	החכם לב—The wise of heart
HER BLESSING	She will use her wisdom and spirituality to pursue the peace of the dove.

YEMINAH ימינה

VARIANT	Yemina
HEBREW	Right hand, strength
GEMATRIA	115
HER WORD	יעלה—Will go up (Gen. 2:6)
HER PHRASE	ידי אמן—Hands of an artisan
HER BLESSING	She will rise in all her endeavours because of her strength and craftsmanship.

YEPHRA יפרה

HEBREW	Riches, abundance
GEMATRIA	295
HER WORD	פריה*—Her fruit (Lev. 25:19)
HER PHRASE	חכמה וגבורה—Wisdom and strength
HER BLESSING	She will be fruitful and multiply. Her wisdom and strength will ensure her success in life.

YERUSHA ירושה

HEBREW	Inheritance
GEMATRIA	521
HER WORD	והישר*—And what is right (Ex. 15:16)
HER PHRASE	בחסד ואמת—With kindness and truth
HER BLESSING	She will always choose the righteous path. Her honesty and gentle manner will ensure success in all that she undertakes.

YESHISHA ישישה

HEBREW	Old
GEMATRIA	625
HER WORD	הריתי—Conceived (Num. 11:12)
HER PHRASE	ברוח הקדש—With prophetic divine spirit
HER BLESSING	From birth to old age, she will manifest special intuition and insight.

YIGAALA יגאלה

HEBREW	To redeem
GEMATRIA	49
HER WORD	ואגדלה—And I will make great (Gen. 12:2)
HER PHRASE	האהבה והאחוה—Love and brotherhood
HER BLESSING	With extra measures of love, she will express greatness as she redeems others from their difficulties.

YISKAH יסכה

HEBREW	Anointed
GEMATRIA	95
HER WORD	יפה—Beautiful (Gen. 12:14)
HER PHRASE	המח והלב—Mind and heart
HER BLESSING	She will be recognized for the beauty of both her brilliance and character.

YISRAELA ישראלה

VARIANT	Israela
HEBREW	Israeli, prince of God
GEMATRIA	546
HER WORD	מצותי—My commandments (Gen. 26:5)
HER PHRASE	על האמת—On truth
HER BLESSING	She will be deeply committed to truth, to law, and to her people.

YOCHEVED יוכבד

HEBREW	Glory of God
GEMATRIA	42
HER WORD	כבודי*—My glory (Gen. 45:13)
HER PHRASE	אהבה וחדוה—Love and rejoicing
HER BLESSING	She will be a happy, loving, and honored person.

YOELA יואלה

VARIANT	Joela
HEBREW	God is willing
GEMATRIA	52
HER WORD	בכל—With everything (Gen. 24:1)
HER PHRASE	יד ולב—Hand and heart
HER BLESSING	To have a caring heart for others and the will to do good with her hands.

YOHANA יוחנה

VARIANTS	Johana, Joanne, Yochana
HEBREW	God is gracious
GEMATRIA	79
HER WORD	מטל—Of the dew (Gen. 27:28)
	במזל—With luck
HER PHRASE	כל אוהבה—All those who love her
HER BLESSING	She will be successful in all that she undertakes. She will shower her kindness on others and will always be surrounded by love.

YONANAH יוננה

HEBREW	She is graced
GEMATRIA	121
HER WORD	וחזק—And mighty (Ex. 19:19)
HER PHRASE	כל מאודך—All of your might
HER BLESSING	Graced with strength and fortitude, she will overcome every obstacle in life.

YORIT יורית

VARIANT	Jorit
HEBREW	Autumn rain
GEMATRIA	626
HER WORD	הראתך—Show you (Ex. 9:16)
HER PHRASE	חכמת נבונים—The wisdom of the intelligent
HER BLESSING	She will be a shining example to all. Her intelligence will lead her to wise choices in life.

YOSEPHA יוספה

HEBREW	God will add
GEMATRIA	161
HER WORD	ונעלה—And go up (Gen. 35:3)
HER PHRASE	קול חיבה—The voice of love
HER BLESSING	God will add to her blessings and allow her to ascend to greater heights in reward for her loving words.

YOVELAH יובלה

VARIANT	Yovela
HEBREW	Jubilee, rejoicing
GEMATRIA	53
HER WORD	היובל*—The jubilee year (Lev. 25:13)
HER PHRASE	בא גואלי—My redeemer has come
HER BLESSING	Like the jubilee year, she brings the blessings of freedom, redemption, and material fulfillment.

Z

ZAKA זכה

HEBREW	Bright, pure, clear
GEMATRIA	32
HER WORD	לב—Heart (Gen. 8:21)
HER PHRASE	אחד האהוב—The beloved one
HER BLESSING	She will draw forth special love because of the purity of her heart.

ZARIZA זריזה

HEBREW	Industrious
GEMATRIA	229
HER WORD	ואברך—And I blessed (Gen. 24:48)
HER PHRASE	מקיים הבטחה—Keeps one's promise
HER BLESSING	She speedily keeps her word and for this receives God's blessings.

ZAYIT זית

HEBREW	Olive
GEMATRIA	417
HER WORD	הבית—House (Gen. 19:4)
HER PHRASE	יום הכפורים—The day of atonement
HER BLESSING	Her house is her castle, her nature is forgiving, and she is as giving as the olive tree.

ZAZA זזה

HEBREW	Movement
GEMATRIA	19
HER WORD	בטוב—In the best (Gen. 20:15)
HER PHRASE	החג בא—The holiday comes
HER BLESSING	She will bring the festiveness of the holidays to her friends and family with her every movement.

ZEFIRAH זפירה

HEBREW	Crown
GEMATRIA	302
HER WORD	בקר—Morning (Gen. 1:5)
HER PHRASE	יהללך זר—A stranger will praise you
HER BLESSING	Crowned with the glory of morning, she will elicit praise even from strangers.

ZEHAVA זהבה

VARIANT	Zahava
HEBREW	To shine, light, brightness
GEMATRIA	19
HER WORD	הזהב*—The gold (Gen. 2:11)
HER PHRASE	החג בא—The holiday comes
HER BLESSING	She will shine with the brightness of the festivals and be treasured like gold.

ZEHIRA זהירה

HEBREW	Guarded, protected
GEMATRIA	227
HER WORD	ברכה—Blessing (Gen. 12:2)
HER PHRASE	טוב לעניים—Good to the poor
HER BLESSING	She will be exceedingly charitable and protective of others, for which she will be blessed.

ZELYA זליה

HEBREW	Zealous, ardent
GEMATRIA	52
HER WORD	בכל—With everything (Gen. 16:12)
HER PHRASE	אבא ואמא—Father and mother
HER BLESSING	She will ardently honor her parents in every way and her zealousness will be blessed.

ZEPHIRAH צפירה

VARIANT	Tzephirah
HEBREW	Morning
GEMATRIA	385
HER WORD	הרקיע—The firmament (Gen 1:7)
HER PHRASE	לעיני כל העמים—To the eyes of all the nations
HER BLESSING	She will achieve universal renown as a pioneering trailblazer.

ZETA זיתה

HEBREW	An olive
GEMATRIA	422
HER WORD	ביתי—My house (Gen. 15:2)
HER PHRASE	יש לה מזל—She has good fortune
HER BLESSING	She will have extremely good fortune in family matters.

ZEVIDA זבידה

HEBREW	A gift
GEMATRIA	28
HER WORD	כח—Power (Num. 14:17)
HER PHRASE	די זהב—Sufficient gold
HER BLESSING	Her power will be contentment with what she has; her gift to appreciate what God has given her.

ZEVULA זבולה

HEBREW	A dwelling place, palace
GEMATRIA	50
HER WORD	כל—Everything (Gen. 1:21)
HER PHRASE	כיבוד האב—Parental honor
HER BLESSING	She will always make her dwelling place special by her respect for the past.

ZIA זיע

HEBREW	To tremble
GEMATRIA	87
HER WORD	ויהללו—And they praised (Gen. 12:15)
HER PHRASE	עד אחד—One witness
HER BLESSING	She will be trusted by all and praised for her honesty.

ZILPAH זלפה

HEBREW	Dripping, sprinkling
GEMATRIA	122
HER WORD	בניכם—Your children (Ex. 3:22)
HER PHRASE	הילדה החמודה—The delightful maiden
HER BLESSING	She will always enjoy the gift of youthfulness and be especially beloved.

ZIMRA זמרה

HEBREW	A branch of choice fruits, song of praise
GEMATRIA	252
HER WORD	המאור—The Light (Gen 1:16)
HER PHRASE	הקל הגבור—The mighty God
HER BLESSING	She will bring enlightenment to others and allow them to see the might of God.

ZIRA זירה

HEBREW	An arena
GEMATRIA	222
HER WORD	ברך—Bless (Gen. 22:17)
HER PHRASE	סוף כבודה לבוא—The end of her honor due is yet to come
HER BLESSING	She will be granted ever greater honor and respect as she gets on in years.

ZISSA זיסה

YIDDISH	Sweet one
GEMATRIA	82
HER WORD	ומלאה—And her fullness, her completeness (Deut. 33:16)
HER PHRASE	בלב חם—With a warm heart
HER BLESSING	Warmth, sweetness, and compassion make her a truly complete person

ZIVA זיוה

HEBREW	Brightness, splendor
GEMATRIA	28
HER WORD	ידיד—Beloved (Deut. 33:12)
HER PHRASE	אהבה באהבה—Love in love
HER BLESSING	She will radiate love and friendship and be a magnet for close companions.

ZOHAR זוהר

HEBREW	Light, brilliance
GEMATRIA	218
HER WORD	בצלמנו—In our (divine) image (Gen. 1:26)
HER PHRASE	וענני כבוד—And clouds of glory
HER BLESSING	She will radiate the divine image and be protected by God's constant presence.

ZOHERET זוהרת

HEBREW	She shines
GEMATRIA	618
HER WORD	הבריאת—The healthy ones (Gen. 41:20)
HER PHRASE	טוב תאר—Beautiful of form
HER BLESSING	She will be especially blessed with beauty and health.

MASCULINE NAMES

ABBA אבא

HEBREW	Father
GEMATRIA	4
HIS WORD	אבא*—I will come (Gen. 33:14)
HIS PHRASE	אב "א"—"One" (God) is the Father
HIS BLESSING	He will be deeply attached to his parents and to God. He will always respond quickly when called.

ABIR אביר

HEBREW	Strong, courageous
GEMATRIA	213
HIS WORD	ביאר*—In the river (Ex. 7:17)
HIS PHRASE	בגומלי חסדים—Amongst the doers of acts of kindness
HIS BLESSING	Like the river which hid and protected Moses, he will courageously help others throughout his life.

ACHAV אחאב

VARIANT	Ahab
HEBREW	Father's brother
GEMATRIA	12
HIS WORD	חבב—He loves (Deut. 33:3)
HIS PHRASE	אבא אהב—Father loved
HIS BLESSING	He will be the special delight of his father.

ACHIEZER אחיעזר

HEBREW	My brother is my helper
GEMATRIA	296
HIS WORD	פריו—His fruit (Lev. 19:23)
HIS PHRASE	אור לגוים—A light to the nations
HIS BLESSING	His talents will bear fruit as a blessing to the world at large. He will always be ready to help others.

ACHINOAM אחינועם

HEBREW	My brother is charming
GEMATRIA	185
HIS WORD	הפנים—The face (Ex. 35:13)
HIS PHRASE	אני לדודי ודודי לי—I am for my beloved and my beloved is for me
HIS BLESSING	His extra measure of charm and beauty of face will bless him with the strongest measure of love.

ACHIYA אחיה

HEBREW	God is my brother
GEMATRIA	24
HIS WORD	ויאהב—And he loved (Gen. 25:28)
HIS PHRASE	זה הוא—This is the one
HIS BLESSING	He will be chosen to lead as a true and constant friend.

ADAM אדם

HEBREW	Earth
GEMATRIA	45
HIS WORD	מאד*—Very much, excess (Gen. 1:33)
HIS PHRASE	ידיד טוב—A good friend
HIS BLESSING	His gift for friendship will bring him an excess of blessing. He will be unique, different, and special.

ADAR אדר

HEBREW	Dark, noble, exalted
GEMATRIA	205
HIS WORD	*ארד—I will descend (Gen. 37:35)
HIS PHRASE	*ה' יגן עליו—God will protect him
	(ה is the four letter name of God equaling 26)
HIS BLESSING	In the darkest of times, God will descend and offer him special divine protection.

ADI עדי

HEBREW	A jewel
GEMATRIA	84
HIS WORD	*ידע—Knew (Gen. 4:1)
HIS PHRASE	בכל לב—With full heart
HIS BLESSING	Merging intellect and heart, he will be acknowledged as a jewel among his peers.

ADIR אדיר

HEBREW	Lord, noble, majestic
GEMATRIA	215
HIS WORD	גביר—Lord, ruler (Gen. 27:29)
HIS PHRASE	דיין נאמן—Faithful judge
	אבא אהב—Father loved
HIS BLESSING	He will be the special delight of his father.

ADIV אדיב

ARABIC	Pleasant, gently mannered
GEMATRIA	17
HIS WORD	טוב—Good (Gen. 1:4)
HIS PHRASE	אב אהוב—Beloved father
HIS BLESSING	He will be especially beloved by his children because of his goodness. He will be an excellent parent and teacher.

ADMON אדמון

HEBREW	Red peony flower
GEMATRIA	101
HIS WORD	אכלכל—I will provide, sustain (Gen. 50:21)
HIS PHRASE	טוב מכל לב—Good with all of his heart
HIS BLESSING	He will help and support others because of the goodness of his heart.

ADONIYAH אדוניה

HEBREW	God is my Lord
GEMATRIA	76
HIS WORD	עבד—Workman (Gen. 4:2)
HIS PHRASE	דוגמא טובה—A good example
HIS BLESSING	He will be held up as an inspiration to others faithfully serving God with all his heart.

ADRIEL עדריאל

HEBREW	God is my majesty
GEMATRIA	315
HIS WORD	הקיר—The Wall (Ex. 14:37)
HIS PHRASE	לטובה ולברכה—For good and for blessing
HIS BLESSING	Strength and determination are his traits. Firm and decisive, he will be a source of goodness and blessing.

AHARON אהרן

VARIANT	Aaron
HEBREW	Teaching, singing, shining, mountain
GEMATRIA	256
HIS WORD	הארן*—The ark (Ex. 25:14)
HIS PHRASE	בן צדק—Son of a righteous one
HIS BLESSING	He will perpetuate the spiritual values of his ancestors.

AKIVA עקיבא

VARIANT	Akiba
HEBREW	Supplant, hold by the heel, or protect
GEMATRIA	183
HIS WORD	נגפים—To be smitten (Deut. 28:7)
	המצליח—The successful one
HIS PHRASE	ללמוד חכמה—To learn wisdom
HIS BLESSING	Through knowledge and wisdom, he will attain extraordinary success. He will become more and more successful with the passage of years.

ALEKSANDER אלכסנדר

VARIANT	Alexander
HEBREW	Protector of men
GEMATRIA	365
HIS WORD	השכם—Rise up early (Ex. 8:16)
HIS PHRASE	בגאולה הקרובה—With the redemption that is near
HIS BLESSING	He will always be first to act and to protect others.

ALON אלון

HEBREW	Oak tree
GEMATRIA	87
HIS WORD	ולהבדיל—And to separate (Gen. 1:18)
HIS PHRASE	כל הכבוד—All honor
HIS BLESSING	He will be especially honored and revered because of his strength of character.

ALTER אלתר

YIDDISH	Old one
GEMATRIA	631
HIS WORD	תאריך—You will prolong (Deut. 4:40)
HIS PHRASE	המבדיל בין קדש לחול—Who separates the holy and the profane
HIS BLESSING	His gift is to be able to distinguish between what is valuable and what is worthless—this talent enables him to prolong his days.

ALUF אלוף

VARIANT	Aluph
HEBREW	Leader, prince, head, chief
GEMATRIA	117
HIS WORD	ואלף*—And a thousand (Num. 3:50)
HIS PHRASE	בכל מאדך—With all your might, with all your possessions
HIS BLESSING	He will be considered unique amongst thousands.

AMATZ אמץ

HEBREW	Strong, courageous
GEMATRIA	131
HIS WORD	מצא*—And he found (Gen. 2:20)
HIS PHRASE	האהבה והאמונה—Love and faith
HIS BLESSING	He will demonstrate the joy of a life that has found love and faith. He will be blessed with special strength and courage.

AMI עמי

HEBREW	My people
GEMATRIA	120
HIS WORD	למלך—To the king (Gen. 40:1)
HIS PHRASE	מזל גדול—Great good fortune
HIS BLESSING	His life will be blessed with luck and good fortune fit for a king.

AMICHAI עמיחי

HEBREW	My folk is alive
GEMATRIA	138
HIS WORD	בקול—With a voice (Gen. 39:14)
HIS PHRASE	דיצה וחדוה—Rejoicing and happiness
HIS BLESSING	He will be a happy person, constantly lifting his voice in song.

AMIEL עמיאל

HEBREW	God of my people
GEMATRIA	151
HIS WORD	מקוה—Waters of purification (Ex. 7:19)
HIS PHRASE	גומל חסד—Doing acts of kindness
HIS BLESSING	He will inspire and purify others through his noble acts of kindness.

AMIKAM עמיקם

HEBREW	My nation has arisen; my nation has been resurrected
GEMATRIA	260
HIS WORD	הגברים—The mighty men (Gen. 6:4)
HIS PHRASE	גדול וגבור—Great and mighty
HIS BLESSING	His strength of character will make him great and mighty.

AMINADAV עמינדב

HEBREW	My nation is noble
GEMATRIA	176
HIS WORD	לקום—To rise up (Gen. 31:35)
HIS PHRASE	יהודי מאמין—A believing Jew
HIS BLESSING	He will always rise from his difficulties to demonstrate the nobility of a believing Jew.

AMIR אמיר

HEBREW	Mighty, strong
GEMATRIA	251
HIS WORD	יאמר*—He will say (Gen. 10:9)
HIS PHRASE	בחכמה העליונה—With higher wisdom
HIS BLESSING	He will be blessed with divine intuition and wisdom endowing his words with special significance.

AMIRAM עמירם

HEBREW	My nation is exalted
GEMATRIA	360
HIS WORD	שִׁמְךָ—Your name, your fame (Gen. 12:2)
HIS PHRASE	רוח חכמה ובינה—A spirit of wisdom and understanding
HIS BLESSING	With his understanding, his name will become famous. He will bring credit to his people.

AMITAN אמתן

HEBREW	True, faithful friend
GEMATRIA	491
HIS WORD	מאנת*—You will refuse (Ex. 10:3)
HIS PHRASE	שלום ומנוחה—Peace and rest
HIS BLESSING	He will be able to stand firm against unworthy temptations, allowing him to find peace and personal contentment.

AMMITAI אמתי

HEBREW	Truth
GEMATRIA	451
HIS WORD	מאתי*—From me (Gen. 44:28)
HIS PHRASE	אמונה של איוב—The faith of Job
HIS BLESSING	He will derive an extra measure of faith from God Himself allowing him to transcend all of his difficulties.

AMNON אמנון

HEBREW	Faithful
GEMATRIA	147
HIS WORD	ויצלהו—And he saved him (Gen. 37:21)
HIS PHRASE	אין כמוך—There is none like you
HIS BLESSING	He will be especially protected and delivered by God because there is no one who can compare with his unique talents.

AMOS עמוס

HEBREW	To be burdened or troubled
GEMATRIA	176
HIS WORD	לקום—To rise up (Gen. 31:35)
HIS PHRASE	יהודי מאמין—A believing Jew
HIS BLESSING	No matter how burdened, he will rise up and overcome.

ANAN ענן

HEBREW	Cloud, soothsayer
GEMATRIA	170
HIS WORD	לעלם—Forever (Gen. 3:22)
HIS PHRASE	בכל יום ויום—Every day
HIS BLESSING	His secret will be to accomplish every single day for every day of his life. He will have gifts of insight and an almost mystical perception of reality.

ARAD ארד

HEBREW	Bronze
GEMATRIA	205
HIS WORD	גבר—Mighty (Gen. 10:8)
HIS PHRASE	קול הנבואה—The voice of prophecy
HIS BLESSING	He will be blessed with intuitive prowess and mighty insights.

ARDON ארדון

HEBREW	Bronze
GEMATRIA	261
HIS WORD	הדברים—The words (Gen. 15:1)
HIS PHRASE	ענו מכל אדם—Most modest of all mankind
HIS BLESSING	He will—with humility—find his words accepted by others.

A R E L   אראל

HEBREW	Icon of God—strong, brave
GEMATRIA	232
HIS WORD	הברכה—The blessing (Gen. 27:41)
HIS PHRASE	נאה לעולם—Beautiful to the world
HIS BLESSING	His courage and bravery will make him blessed and honored by the world.

A R I   ארי

HEBREW	Lion
GEMATRIA	211
HIS WORD	ראי*—Of seeing (Gen. 16:13)
HIS PHRASE	אדם עליון—A lofty person
HIS BLESSING	His strength will rest in his ability to see what others cannot.

A R I E L   אריאל

HEBREW	Lion of God
GEMATRIA	242
HIS WORD	ברכך—Has blessed you (Deut. 2:7)
HIS PHRASE	בדעה צלולה—With clear knowledge
HIS BLESSING	Clarity of thought will be his special gift ensuring his blessing.

A R M O N   ארמון

HEBREW	Castle, palace
GEMATRIA	297
HIS WORD	עזרך—Your help (Deut. 33:29)
HIS PHRASE	אדם רך לב—A soft hearted person
HIS BLESSING	He will be blessed with an extra measure of sensitivity and compassion, helping others in need.

ARNON ארנון

HEBREW	Roaring stream
GEMATRIA	307
HIS WORD	הבקר—The morning (Gen. 44:3)
HIS PHRASE	בעיני כל העם—In the eyes of all the people
HIS BLESSING	Like the brightness of morning, he will be blessed by all. He will love to travel, finding joy in the newness of every morning.

ARYEH אריה

VARIANTS	Arye, Aryeih
HEBREW	Lion
GEMATRIA	216
HIS WORD	ייראה*—He will revere (Gen. 22:14)
HIS PHRASE	אלקים עמך—God is with you
HIS BLESSING	He will revere God and God will respond with His love and protection. He will be blessed with an especially spiritual nature.

ASA אסא

HEBREW	Physician, healer
GEMATRIA	62
HIS WORD	המזבח—Altar (Gen. 13:4)
HIS PHRASE	במח חד—With sharp mind
HIS BLESSING	His acute intellect will be used to help heal others. He will turn to the study of medicine or psychology.

ASAF אסף

VARIANT	Asaph
HEBREW	To gather
GEMATRIA	141
HIS WORD	מלאכים—Angels (Gen. 32:4)
HIS PHRASE	לעבדך באהבה—To serve you with love
HIS BLESSING	With angelic fervor, he will gather people together to serve God with love. He will acquire much knowledge and be known for his wide range of interests.

ASHER אָשֵׁר

HEBREW	Blessed, fortunate, happy
GEMATRIA	501
HIS WORD	ראש*—Head, chief (Gen. 3:15)
HIS PHRASE	עתיד טוב—A good future
HIS BLESSING	His life will progressively get better. He will be happy and blessed, and will have an optimistic nature.

ASIR אסיר

HEBREW	To bind, imprison
GEMATRIA	271
HIS WORD	למאר—To give light (Ex. 25:6)
HIS PHRASE	האספו ואגידה לכם—Gather together and I will tell you
HIS BLESSING	He will be blessed with intuitive insight to enlighten others. He will bind others to him in lifelong friendship.

ATAR עתר

HEBREW	He prayed
GEMATRIA	670
HIS WORD	ערת*—Skins (Gen. 27:16)
HIS PHRASE	צדיקים אומרים מאט—The righteous say little
HIS BLESSING	With few words he will convey important truths. His prayer will be especially favored by God.

ATZMON עצמון

HEBREW	Strength
GEMATRIA	256
HIS WORD	הארן—The ark (Ex. 25:14)
HIS PHRASE	חכם פקח—A shrewd wise person
HIS BLESSING	With strength and intelligence he will be the focus of attention on the ark in the temple.

AVI אבי

HEBREW	My father
GEMATRIA	13
HIS WORD	אחד—One (Gen. 1:5)
HIS PHRASE	בא אבוא—I will surely come
HIS BLESSING	His word will be his bond. He will be gifted at bringing about unity within his family and his community.

AVIAD אביעד

HEBREW	My father is eternal
GEMATRIA	87
HIS WORD	ויהללו—And they praised (Gen. 12:15)
HIS PHRASE	כל הכבוד—All honor
HIS BLESSING	He will be commonly praised and honored.

AVICHAI אביחי

HEBREW	My father is alive
GEMATRIA	31
HIS WORD	הכבוד—The Honor, the glory (Gen. 31:1)
HIS PHRASE	אודה י-ה—I will give thanks to God
HIS BLESSING	He will be grateful to God for all his blessings and in return be rewarded with honor.

AVIDOR אבידור

HEBREW	Father of a generation
GEMATRIA	223
HIS WORD	אברך—I will bless (Gen. 41:43)
HIS PHRASE	מאמונה ובטחון—From faith and trust
HIS BLESSING	God will bless him for his faith and trust with exceptional children.

AVIEZER אביעזר

HEBREW	My father is my help
GEMATRIA	290
HIS WORD	רעך—Your friend (Lev. 19:13)
HIS PHRASE	ומה רב טובך—And how great is your goodness
HIS BLESSING	The ability to be a good friend and helper is his special blessing.

AVIGDOR אביגדור

HEBREW	Father, protector
GEMATRIA	226
HIS WORD	ויחבר—And he joined together, he united (Ex. 36:10)
HIS PHRASE	קול מלך—A kingly voice
HIS BLESSING	With regal force, he will serve to unite and protect others.

AVIMELECH אבימלך

HEBREW	Father of the king, my father is the king
GEMATRIA	103
HIS WORD	הכוכבים—The stars (Gen. 1:16)
HIS PHRASE	החן היהודי—Jewish charm
HIS BLESSING	With a special measure of charm, he will shine like the stars among men.

AVINADOV אבינדב

HEBREW	Generous father
GEMATRIA	69
HIS WORD	לאחיך—For your brother (Gen. 20:16)
HIS PHRASE	לאהבה ואחוה—For love and brotherhood
HIS BLESSING	He will excel in interpersonal relationships with friends and family.

AVINOAM אבינעם

HEBREW	Father of delight
GEMATRIA	173
HIS WORD	וזקני—And the elders (Ex. 3:18)
HIS PHRASE	קול אבי הוא זה—This is the voice of my father
HIS BLESSING	He will link the past to the future, serving as a reminder of his elders to his own children.

AVIRAM אבירם

HEBREW	My father is mighty
GEMATRIA	253
HIS WORD	להריח—To perfume, to make pleasant the odor (Ex. 30:38)
HIS PHRASE	מהולל בפי כל—Praised by the mouths of all
HIS BLESSING	His presence will be welcomed by everyone and he will be praised by them.

AVISHUR אבישור

VARIANT	Abishur
HEBREW	My father is upright, my father is a wall (dependable)
GEMATRIA	519
HIS WORD	והתיצבו—And they will stand (Num. 11:16)
HIS PHRASE	אל תדאג כלל—Do not worry at all
HIS BLESSING	He will stand firm, without fear, throughout his life. He will be dependable and trustworthy.

AVITAL אביטל

HEBREW	Father of dew
GEMATRIA	52
HIS WORD	בכל—With everything (Gen. 9:2)
HIS PHRASE	יד ולב—Hand and heart
HIS BLESSING	He will be gifted both in his deeds and his thoughts, being sensitive as well as practical.

AVIV אביב

HEBREW	Spring, youthfulness
GEMATRIA	15
HIS WORD	גבהה—High (Deut. 3:5)
HIS PHRASE	או אז—Or then
HIS BLESSING	If not immediately, he will find youthful blessings in later life.

AVNER אבנר

VARIANT	Abner
HEBREW	Father of light
GEMATRIA	253
HIS WORD	ואמרו—And they will say (Gen. 12:12)
HIS PHRASE	החכם בין חכמים—The wise one amongst the wise
HIS BLESSING	He will stand out amongst his peers for his intellect.

AVRAHAM אברהם

VARIANT	Abraham
HEBREW	Exalted father, father of a mighty nation
GEMATRIA	248
HIS WORD	הבראם*—When they were created (Gen. 5:2)
HIS PHRASE	בצלם אלקים—In the image of God
HIS BLESSING	He will personify the image of God as illustrated by the first Jew. He will be a natural leader with the ability to influence others

AVSHALOM אבשלום

VARIANT	Absalom
HEBREW	Father of peace
GEMATRIA	379
HIS WORD	בהקריבכם—When you will bring a sacrifice (Num. 28:26)
HIS PHRASE	כח הרצון—The power of will
HIS BLESSING	With will power and self-sacrifice, he will achieve all of his goals.

AYAL אייל

HEBREW	Deer, ram
GEMATRIA	51
HIS WORD	נא—Please now (Gen. 12:11)
HIS PHRASE	אחד ויחיד—One and unique
HIS BLESSING	He will speedily carry out his obligations and be recognised as a unique individual.

AZARYAH עזריה

HEBREW	God helps
GEMATRIA	292
HIS WORD	מברכיך—Those who bless you (Gen. 12:3)
HIS PHRASE	הוא זכור לטוב—He is remembered for good
HIS BLESSING	His contributions will be lasting and he will be blessed by future generations.

AZI עזי

HEBREW	Strong
GEMATRIA	87
HIS WORD	ויהללו—And they praised (Gen. 12:15)
HIS PHRASE	כל הכבוד—All honor
HIS BLESSING	His accomplishments will elicit praise and honor. His strength of character will define his uniqueness.

AZRIEL עזריאל

HEBREW	God is my help
GEMATRIA	318
HIS WORD	וישב—And he returned (Gen. 4:16)
HIS PHRASE	כבנים הנאמנים—Like faithful children
HIS BLESSING	He will always return to his roots and be faithful to his heritage.

B

BARAK ברק

HEBREW	Flash of light
GEMATRIA	302
HIS WORD	בֹּקֶר*—Morning (Gen. 1:5)
HIS PHRASE	הלכה כדבריו—The law is as his words
HIS BLESSING	With the illumination of morning and the clarity of a lightning flash, his words carry the imprint of truth and deserve to be followed.

BARAM ברעם

HEBREW	Son of the nation
GEMATRIA	312
HIS WORD	חדש—New (Ex. 1:8)
HIS PHRASE	אור ליהודים—A light to the Jews
HIS BLESSING	His new insights and ideas will bring light to our people.

BAREL בר-אל

HEBREW	Son of God
GEMATRIA	233
HIS WORD	זכור—Remember (Ex. 13:3)
HIS PHRASE	כמליץ גדול—As a great interceder
HIS BLESSING	His excellent memory will make him a fine negotiator.

BARTHOLOMEW ברתלמי

HEBREW	Hill, furrow
GEMATRIA	682
HIS WORD	ברכתני—Bless me (Gen. 32:27)
HIS PHRASE	למד זכות על יהודים—Judges fellow Jews favorably
HIS BLESSING	Always seeking to find goodness in others, he will be blessed with favor.

BARUCH ברוך

HEBREW	Blessed
GEMATRIA	228
HIS WORD	בכרו*—His firstborn (Gen. 10:15)
HIS PHRASE	הכח נעלם—The hidden power
HIS BLESSING	With a concealed inner strength, he will be first amongst his peers to do good and be blessed. He will be a pioneer, breaking new ground with his creativity and his daring personality.

BARZILAI ברזלי

HEBREW	Man of iron
GEMATRIA	249
HIS WORD	ואברכך—And I will bless you (Gen. 12:2)
HIS PHRASE	אדם צדיק—A righteous person
HIS BLESSING	With the firmness of iron, he will lead a life of righteousness and receive divine blessing.

BAZAK בזק

HEBREW	Lightning (quick as)
GEMATRIA	109
HIS WORD	מנוחה—A resting place (Num. 10:33)
HIS PHRASE	גמול ידיו—The reward of his hands
HIS BLESSING	He will perform his tasks speedily, allowing him ample time for rest and reward for his efforts.

BEN-AMI בֶּן-עַמִּי

HEBREW	Son of my people
GEMATRIA	172
HIS WORD	בענן—In the cloud (Gen. 9:13)
HIS PHRASE	בעל סוד—Master of secrets
HIS BLESSING	Blessed with a spiritual and mystical nature, he will probe the secrets of the heavens.

BENJAMIN בְּנִימִין

VARIANT	Benyamin
HEBREW	Son of my right hand
GEMATRIA	162
HIS WORD	בצלם—In the image (Gen. 1:27)
HIS PHRASE	חן וכבוד *מה׳—Charm and glory from God (ה׳ refers to God's four letter name equaling 26)
HIS BLESSING	Possessed of an extra measure of charm and charisma, he will be perceived in the image of God.

BEN-TZIYON בֶּנְצִיּוֹן

HEBREW	Son of Zion, excellent son
GEMATRIA	208
HIS WORD	ארבה—I will increase (Gen. 3:16)
HIS PHRASE	מכלכל חיים—Supporter of life
HIS BLESSING	He will be enabled to support others, spiritually and financially

BEREKHYAH בְּרֶכְיָה

HEBREW	Blessed of the Lord
GEMATRIA	237
HIS WORD	לאור—For light (Gen. 1:5)
HIS PHRASE	החבר הטוב—The good friend
HIS BLESSING	He will be blessed by God because of his friendship to others.

BERIAH בריאה

HEBREW	Creature
GEMATRIA	218
HIS WORD	ריח—Sweet savor (Gen. 8:21)
HIS PHRASE	כיועץ הטוב—Like a good advisor
HIS BLESSING	His advice will be treasured and his company will be desired.

BETZALEIL בצלאל

VARIANT	Betzalel
HEBREW	In the shadow of God
GEMATRIA	153
HIS WORD	בחפזון—In haste (Ex. 12:11)
HIS PHRASE	נאמן הוא—He is trustworthy
HIS BLESSING	He will quickly carry out his promises.

BILDAD בלדד

HEBREW	Beloved
GEMATRIA	40
HIS WORD	חלב—Fat, the best (Gen. 45:18)
HIS PHRASE	אוהב ה'*—Friend of God
	(ה' refers to God's four letter name equaling 26)
HIS BLESSING	He will be beloved by man and by God. He will sacrifice "the fat," the best, of his possessions for his friends and for God.

BOAZ בעז

HEBREW	Strength, swiftness
GEMATRIA	79
HIS WORD	עזב*—Left (Gen. 24:27)
HIS PHRASE	הביטו אליו—Look at him
HIS BLESSING	He will be a role model for others because of his strength of character.

C

CALEB כלב

HEBREW	Heart or dog
ARABIC	Bold, brave
GEMATRIA	52
HIS WORD	בכל*—With everything (Gen. 9:2)
HIS PHRASE	יד ולב—Hand and heart
HIS BLESSING	He will combine the strength of his hand with the goodness of his heart to serve God and man.

CARMEL כרמל

VARIANT	Carmi
HEBREW	Vineyard, farm, garden
GEMATRIA	290
HIS WORD	רעך—Your friend (Ex. 2:13)
HIS PHRASE	ומה רב טובך—And how great is your goodness
HIS BLESSING	With great goodness he will acquire many friends.

CHABIBI חביבי

VARIANTS	Chavivi, Habibi, Havivi
HEBREW	My beloved
GEMATRIA	32
HIS WORD	לב—Heart (Gen. 8:21)
HIS PHRASE	אחד ואחד—One by one
HIS BLESSING	He will be a master of interpersonal relationships, beloved for his good heart.

CHAGAI חגי

VARIANT	Hagai
HEBREW	My celebration
GEMATRIA	21
HIS WORD	אחזה—A possession (Gen. 47:11)
HIS PHRASE	בחג הבא—In the coming holiday
HIS BLESSING	His days will be filled with joyous festive occasions.

CHALIL חליל

VARIANT	Halil
HEBREW	Flute
GEMATRIA	78
HIS WORD	חלם—Dreaming (Gen. 41:1)
HIS PHRASE	לב האם—Heart of the mother
HIS BLESSING	He will have a very sensitive and poetic nature. He will enjoy music, the arts, and cultural activities.

CHAMIYAH חמיה

VARIANT	Hamiyah
HEBREW	God's warmth
GEMATRIA	63
HIS WORD	נביא—Prophet (Gen. 20:7)
HIS PHRASE	באהבה גדולה—With great love
HIS BLESSING	With much love he will be divinely inspired to bring God's warmth to the world.

CHANAN חנן

VARIANT	Hanan
HEBREW	He was compassionate
GEMATRIA	108
HIS WORD	נבון—Understanding (Gen. 41:33)
HIS PHRASE	הלב מלא—The heart is full
HIS BLESSING	Blessed with understanding and compassion, he will allow the fullness of his heart to overflow with good deeds for others.

CHANANIA חנניה

VARIANT	Hanania
HEBREW	The compassion of God
GEMATRIA	123
HIS WORD	הנחני*—Has led me (Gen. 24:48)
HIS PHRASE	כל הכבוד לו—All honor is due him
HIS BLESSING	His life will be marked by clear moments of divine compassion, guidance, and intervention.

CHANOCH חנוך

VARIANT	Enoch
HEBREW	Dedicated; educated and raised correctly
GEMATRIA	84
HIS WORD	ידע—Knows (Gen. 3:5)
HIS PHRASE	הוא יבין—He will comprehend
HIS BLESSING	Highly educated, he will be a profound thinker and scholar.

CHASDAI חסדאי

VARIANT	Hasdai
HEBREW	Righteous
GEMATRIA	83
HIS WORD	והחסד—And mercy (Deut. 7:9)
HIS PHRASE	בו בוטחים—In him they trust
HIS BLESSING	He will inspire trust and confidence in others because of his righteousness.

CHAVAKUK חבקוק

VARIANT	Havakuk
HEBREW	Embrace
GEMATRIA	216
HIS WORD	יראה—Reverance, awe (Gen. 22:14)
HIS PHRASE	בבעלי אמונה—Amongst those who master faith
HIS BLESSING	He embraces faith with reverence and awe.

CHAYIM חיים

VARIANT	Hayim
HEBREW	Life
GEMATRIA	68
HIS WORD	ויבן—And he built (Gen. 2:22)
HIS PHRASE	כחו היה בזה—His power was here
HIS BLESSING	He will build projects for the future that will ensure him life beyond his days on earth.

CHILKIYA חלקיה

VARIANT	Hilkiya
HEBREW	God's portion
GEMATRIA	153
HIS WORD	בחפזון—With haste (Ex. 12:11)
HIS PHRASE	יסוד החיים—The secret of life
HIS BLESSING	He will quickly master the most important truths of life.

CHIRAM חירם

VARIANT	Hiram
HEBREW	Freeborn, noble
GEMATRIA	258
HIS WORD	רחים*—The mill (Deut. 24:6)
HIS PHRASE	כאומן נאמן—As a trustworthy artisan
HIS BLESSING	His work and his unique craftsmanship will make him noble.

CHISDA חסדא

VARIANT	Hisda
HEBREW	Zealous
GEMATRIA	73
HIS WORD	החיים—Life (Gen. 2:9)
HIS PHRASE	זה היום—This very day
HIS BLESSING	His zealous nature will endow every day with special meaning and achievements.

159

CHIZKIYA חזקיה

VARIANT	Hizkiya
HEBREW	Might of God
GEMATRIA	130
HIS WORD	עין—Eye (Ex. 21:24)
HIS PHRASE	זה יפה וטוב—He is beautiful and good
HIS BLESSING	Beauty and strength of character will be his special gifts from God.

CHIZKIYAHU חזקיהו

VARIANT	Hizkiyahu
HEBREW	Strengthened by the Lord
GEMATRIA	136
HIS WORD	קול—Voice (Gen. 3:8)
HIS PHRASE	בלב מבין—With an understanding heart
HIS BLESSING	His voice will be heeded because his words will come from his heart.

CHOFNI חפני

VARIANTS	Chafni, Hafni, Hofni
HEBREW	Fighter, pugilist
GEMATRIA	148
HIS WORD	יצמח—He will sprout (Gen. 2:5)
HIS PHRASE	גדול ליהודים—Great for the Jews
HIS BLESSING	He will fight for his people and become great amongst them.

CHUR חור

VARIANT	Hur
HEBREW	Child
GEMATRIA	214
HIS WORD	רוח*—Spirit, wind (Gen. 6:17)
HIS PHRASE	זמנים טובים—Good times
HIS BLESSING	There will be many special occasions in which he will be blessed with divine spirit and happiness.

D

DAGAN דגן

HEBREW	Corn, grain
GEMATRIA	57
HIS WORD	נגד*—Opposite, facing (Gen. 31:32)
HIS PHRASE	אחד אל אחד—One to one
HIS BLESSING	He will be able to successfully face others in negotiations and persuade them to his way of thinking.

DAN דן

HEBREW	To judge
GEMATRIA	54
HIS WORD	לבבך—Your heart (Gen. 20:6)
HIS PHRASE	אך בטח בו—But trust in him
HIS BLESSING	He will be trusted to judge fairly and honestly. People will place confidence in his decisions.

DANIEL דניאל

VARIANT	Daniyel, Danieil, Danny
HEBREW	God is my judge
GEMATRIA	95
HIS WORD	יפה—Beautiful (Gen. 12:14)
HIS PHRASE	אהבה עזה—Strong love
HIS BLESSING	He will master the art of tough love, being both judgmental and compassionate.

DAR דר

HEBREW	Pearl, mother of pearl
GEMATRIA	204
HIS WORD	רד*—Descend (Ex. 19:21)
HIS PHRASE	בכל הזמנים—At all times
HIS BLESSING	He will be blessed with consistency, always luminous as a pearl.

DATAN דתן

HEBREW	Faith, law
GEMATRIA	454
HIS WORD	תמיד—Always (Ex. 25:30)
HIS PHRASE	חיים שלוים—Peaceful life
HIS BLESSING	He will never veer from the straight path and he will enjoy a life of serenity.

DAVID דוד

HEBREW	Beloved
GEMATRIA	14
HIS WORD	זהב—Gold (Gen. 24:22)
HIS PHRASE	חג בא—A holiday comes
HIS BLESSING	He will be loved and always welcomed, like a much awaited holiday.

DEKEL דקל

ARABIC	Palm or date tree
GEMATRIA	134
HIS WORD	הפליט—Survivor (Gen. 14:13)
HIS PHRASE	לכבוד אביו ואמו—For the honor of his father and mother
HIS BLESSING	He will be a special remnant and reminder of past generations.

DEROR דרור

VARIANT	Dror
HEBREW	Freedom or free flowing, bird (swallow)
GEMATRIA	410
HIS WORD	שמע—Hear (Gen. 21:12)
HIS PHRASE	כי לא אשכחך—For I will not forget you
HIS BLESSING	He will make himself heard and will be unforgettable.

DEVIR דביר

ARABIC	Innermost room, holy place
GEMATRIA	216
HIS WORD	דברי*—The words of (Gen. 24:30)
HIS PHRASE	הוא צדיק—He is righteous
HIS BLESSING	His words will carry special meaning as bearers of righteous and holy ideas.

DODO דודו

HEBREW	Beloved, his uncle
GEMATRIA	20
HIS WORD	ידו—His hand (Gen. 3:22)
HIS PHRASE	אב טוב—A good father
HIS BLESSING	With a firm hand, he will prove to be an ideal parent.

DOR דור

HEBREW	A generation, dwelling
GEMATRIA	210
HIS WORD	רדו*—Go down (Gen. 42:2)
HIS PHRASE	חכם ועניו—Wise and modest
HIS BLESSING	In humility he will descend to assist others and be a blessing to his generation.

DORON דורון

HEBREW	A gift
GEMATRIA	266
HIS WORD	כמראה—Like the appearance (Lev. 13:43)
HIS PHRASE	כצלם אלקים—Like the image of God
HIS BLESSING	He will be a true gift from God, with an almost divine image.

DOSON דתן

VARIANT	Doton
HEBREW	Gift
GEMATRIA	454
HIS WORD	תמיד—Always (Ex. 25:30)
HIS PHRASE	חיים שלוים—Peaceful life
HIS BLESSING	He will enjoy a tranquil life as a special gift from God.

DOV דב

HEBREW	A bear
ARABIC	To walk gently, leisurely
GEMATRIA	6
HIS WORD	בד*—Fine linen (Ex. 28:42)
HIS PHRASE	אב בא—Father comes
HIS BLESSING	He will be a perfect representation of his father.

DOVEV דובב

HEBREW	To speak or whisper
GEMATRIA	14
HIS WORD	זהב—Gold (Lev. 24:22)
HIS PHRASE	חג בא—Holiday comes
HIS BLESSING	His words and even his whispers will be anticipated like a beloved holiday.

D U R I E L דוריאל

HEBREW	My house belongs to God
GEMATRIA	251
HIS WORD	מורה—Teacher (Gen. 12:16)
HIS PHRASE	כי יבנה ויצליח—For he will build and succeed
HIS BLESSING	He will instruct others and be highly successful.

E

EDEN עדן

HEBREW	Delight
GEMATRIA	124
HIS WORD	נדע*—We will know (Gen. 43:7)
HIS PHRASE	בגדול דעה—With great knowledge
HIS BLESSING	His unique intellect will serve as special delight.

EDOM אדום

HEBREW	Red
GEMATRIA	51
HIS WORD	ואדם*—And man, and Adam (Gen. 2:5)
HIS PHRASE	אחד ויחיד—One and unique
HIS BLESSING	Like Adam, the first man, his blessing is his singularity and uniqueness.

EFRAYIM אפרים

VARIANT	Ephraim
HEBREW	Fruitful
GEMATRIA	331
HIS WORD	כאיש*—Like a man (Num. 14:15)
HIS PHRASE	לא ייעף ולא ייגע—He will neither tire nor become weary
HIS BLESSING	With an abundance of energy he will make all his efforts bear fruit.

EHUD אהוד

HEBREW	Union
GEMATRIA	16
HIS WORD	אודה*—I will give thanks (Gen. 29:35)
HIS PHRASE	זה אבא—This one is father
HIS BLESSING	His greatest attribute will be gratitude, never taking his gifts for granted.

EILAM עילם

HEBREW	Eternal
GEMATRIA	150
HIS WORD	קלך—Your voice (Gen. 3:10)
HIS PHRASE	אבטח ולא אפחד—I will trust and not be afraid
HIS BLESSING	With an unflagging voice, he will fearlessly speak words of truth to others.

EILON אילון

HEBREW	Oak tree
GEMATRIA	97
HIS WORD	מלאכו—His angel (Gen. 24:7)
HIS PHRASE	השה אזנך—Inclining your ear
HIS BLESSING	Firmly and forcefully he will express views that people will be anxious to hear.

EITAN איתן

VARIANT	Ittan
HEBREW	Strength
GEMATRIA	461
HIS WORD	אתכם—With you (Gen. 9:9)
HIS PHRASE	חן של חכמה—The charm of intelligence
HIS BLESSING	Exceedingly gifted with charm and wisdom, he will use the strength of his talents to find great closeness with others.

EIVER עבר

HEBREW	To go over
GEMATRIA	272
HIS WORD	ערב*—Evening (Gen. 1:5)
HIS PHRASE	לא ימוט לעולם—He will never be moved
HIS BLESSING	Once he undertakes something, he will see it to its final conclusion.

ELAD אלעד

HEBREW	God is eternal
GEMATRIA	105
HIS WORD	הימים—The days (Gen. 4:10)
HIS PHRASE	ביום ההוא יהיה—In that day it will come to pass
HIS BLESSING	His life will see progression and ever greater growth and fulfillment.

ELAZAR אלעזר

HEBREW	God has helped
GEMATRIA	308
HIS WORD	קרוב—Near (Gen. 45:10)
HIS PHRASE	לעבוד ולקיים—To do and to fulfill
HIS BLESSING	He will draw near to help, and with hard work he will fulfill his goals.

ELCHANAN אלחנן

VARIANT	Elhanan
HEBREW	God has graced
GEMATRIA	139
HIS WORD	ונחלמה—And we dreamed (Gen. 41:11)
HIS PHRASE	להנאה גדולה—For great enjoyment
HIS BLESSING	He will fulfill his dreams for enjoyment and happiness.

E L I   עלי

HEBREW	Uplifted
GEMATRIA	110
HIS WORD	עם—People, nation (Gen. 11:6)
HIS PHRASE	אל אחיכם—To your brothers
HIS BLESSING	He will be dedicated to the needs of his people and committed to the larger goals of his brothers and nation.

E L I E Z E R   אליעזר

HEBREW	My god has helped
GEMATRIA	318
HIS WORD	וישב—And he dwelled, and he returned (Gen. 4:16)
HIS PHRASE	במעלה עליונה—On the highest level
HIS BLESSING	He will live life on the level of greatest expertise.

E L I M E L E C H   אלימלך

HEBREW	My God is king
GEMATRIA	131
HIS WORD	והצל—And he saved (Ex. 5:23)
HIS PHRASE	יגל לבנו—He will make our hearts rejoice
HIS BLESSING	With regal authority, he will be able to help others.

E L I S H A   אלישע

HEBREW	God is my salvation
GEMATRIA	411
HIS WORD	תחג—You will celebrate (Ex. 23:14)
HIS PHRASE	ביום שמחה—On a day of rejoicing
HIS BLESSING	He will enjoy special occasions of divine blessing and salvation.

ELIYAHU אליהו

HEBREW	The Lord is my God
GEMATRIA	52
HIS WORD	בכל—With everything (Gen. 9:2)
HIS PHRASE	יד ולב—Hand and heart
HIS BLESSING	He will combine the talents of hand, heart, skill, and compassion.

ELKANAH אלקנה

HEBREW	God bought
GEMATRIA	186
HIS WORD	פעלו—His work (Deut. 32:4)
HIS PHRASE	חנוך בנים—Educating children
HIS BLESSING	His talents will enable him to teach and inspire the young.

ELRAD אלרד

HEBREW	God is the ruler
GEMATRIA	235
HIS WORD	הכיר—The laver (Ex. 30:28)
HIS PHRASE	רביד הזהב—The golden rod
HIS BLESSING	Leadership and purity are his two major gifts.

ELYAKIM אליקים

VARIANT	Eliakim
HEBREW	God established
GEMATRIA	191
HIS WORD	הצלינו—Saved us (Ex. 2:19)
HIS PHRASE	אכן מזל נדול—Surely he has great good fortune
HIS BLESSING	God established for him a good future with extra measures of *mazel* (good luck).

EMANUEL עמנואל

HEBREW	God is with us
GEMATRIA	197
HIS WORD	ונאמנים—And faithful (Deut. 28:59)
HIS PHRASE	כגן עדן—Like the Garden of Eden
HIS BLESSING	God will be with him as He was in paradise. He will be a faithful friend, mate, and father.

EMMET אמת

HEBREW	Truth
GEMATRIA	441
HIS WORD	אתם*—You (Gen. 29:4)
HIS PHRASE	נודה לשמו—We will give thanks to His name
HIS BLESSING	Truthfulness will be his chief concern, and others will be grateful.

ENOSH אנוש

HEBREW	Man
GEMATRIA	357
HIS WORD	ונקרא—And shall be called (Deut. 25:10)
HIS PHRASE	לחברים טובים—For good friends
HIS BLESSING	He will be called a real man among men, a true friend among friends.

ER ער

HEBREW	Aware
GEMATRIA	270
HIS WORD	רכים—Tender (Gen. 33:13)
HIS PHRASE	קבצנו יחד—Bring us together
HIS BLESSING	Sensitive, tender, and aware, he will unite people who are not at peace with each other.

ERAN ערן

HEBREW	Happy
GEMATRIA	320
HIS WORD	לרעך—To your neighbor (Ex. 20:14)
HIS PHRASE	מרבה חכמה—Increase of wisdom
HIS BLESSING	Blessed with a happy disposition, he will have many friends.

ESHKOL אשכול

HEBREW	A cluster of grapes
GEMATRIA	357
HIS WORD	ושאלך*—And he will ask you (Gen. 32:18)
HIS PHRASE	נאמן ונעמן—Faithful and pleasant
HIS BLESSING	A questioning personality, he will be a true and pleasant companion.

ETZYON עציון

HEBREW	Tree
GEMATRIA	226
HIS WORD	ויחבר—And he joined (Ex. 36:10)
HIS PHRASE	לזווג מוצלח—To a successful partnership
HIS BLESSING	He will find successful partners in both business and marriage.

EVENEZER אבנעזר

VARIANT	Ebenezer
HEBREW	Stone of help
GEMATRIA	330
HIS WORD	לכפר—To atone (Ex. 30:15)
HIS PHRASE	בגיל ורעדה—With fear and trembling
HIS BLESSING	He will help others and gain atonement for them with firmness and discipline.

EYAL אייל

HEBREW	Power, strength
GEMATRIA	51
HIS WORD	נא—Please (Gen. 12:11)
HIS PHRASE	וידיד טוב—And a good friend
HIS BLESSING	A strong friend, with a sensitive and courteous nature.

EZRA עזרא

HEBREW	Help
GEMATRIA	278
HIS WORD	ויברכם—And he blessed them (Gen. 48:20)
HIS PHRASE	אור הגנוז—Hidden light
HIS BLESSING	He will be a source of help with the gift of an inner hidden light.

G

GAD גד

VARIANT	Gadi
ARABIC AND HEBREW	Happy, fortunate, troop, warrior
GEMATRIA	7
HIS WORD	או—Or, if (Gen. 24:49)
	דג*—Fish
HIS PHRASE	אבא בא—Father comes
HIS BLESSING	A happy personality and a fruitful life will be his great gifts.

GADIEL גדיאל

HEBREW	God is my fortune or blessing
GEMATRIA	48
HIS WORD	הגדול—The greatest (Gen. 10:21)
HIS PHRASE	בכח האהבה—With the power of love
HIS BLESSING	He will stand out amongst men by the power of his love.

GADOL גדול

HEBREW	Large
GEMATRIA	43
HIS WORD	דגלו*—His flag (Num. 1:52)
HIS PHRASE	חוזה טוב—A good seer
HIS BLESSING	He will be great and recognizable as one who foresees the future.

GAI גיא

HEBREW	Valley
GEMATRIA	14
HIS WORD	זהב—Gold (Gen. 24:22)
HIS PHRASE	חג בא—A holiday has come
HIS BLESSING	Sparkling and brilliant, his company brings with it the joy of a holiday.

GAL גל

VARIANT	Gali
HEBREW	Wave, mountain, heap
GEMATRIA	33
HIS WORD	יחיה—Shall live (Gen. 31:32)
HIS PHRASE	אהבה אחוה—Love, brotherhood
HIS BLESSING	Wave after wave he shall live many days in reward for his great love.

GALIL גליל

HEBREW	Rolling hills
GEMATRIA	73
HIS WORD	חכמה—Wisdom (Ex. 28:3)
HIS PHRASE	זה היום—This very day
HIS BLESSING	He will, with great wisdom, display perfect timing for his actions.

GAMLIEL גמליאל

HEBREW	God is my reward
GEMATRIA	114
HIS WORD	חנון—Gracious (Ex. 22:26)
HIS PHRASE	ידיד אלקים—Friend of God
HIS BLESSING	His graciousness is his reward from God.

GAN גן

HEBREW	Garden
GEMATRIA	53
HIS WORD	החיל—Wealth (Deut. 8:17)
HIS PHRASE	החוזה הטוב—The good seer
HIS BLESSING	He will be blessed with vision and insight, which will make him wealthy both spiritually and materially.

GAVRIEL גבריאל

HEBREW	God is my strength
GEMATRIA	246
HIS WORD	להאיר—To give light (Gen. 1:15)
HIS PHRASE	ברי לבב—Pure of heart
HIS BLESSING	God will endow him with special strength of character and purity of heart.

GEDALYAH גדליה

VARIANT	Gedalia, Gedalya
HEBREW	God is great
GEMATRIA	52
HIS WORD	בכל—With everything (Gen. 9:2)
HIS PHRASE	יד ולב—Hand and heart
HIS BLESSING	He will have a caring heart for others and the will to do good with his hands.

GEDI גדי

HEBREW	Cub
GEMATRIA	17
HIS WORD	גיד*—The (strong) sinew (Gen. 32:33)
HIS PHRASE	אב אוהב—A loving father
HIS BLESSING	He will be both youthful and strong all of his days.

GEFANIA גפניה

HEBREW	Wine, vineyard of the Lord
GEMATRIA	148
HIS WORD	יצמח—He will sprout (Gen. 2:5)
HIS PHRASE	והוא יכלכלך—And he will support you
HIS BLESSING	He will be blessed with great wealth, enabling him to support those in need.

GERSHOM גרשום

HEBREW	Stranger there
GEMATRIA	549
HIS WORD	העמדתיך—I have made you stand (Ex. 9:16)
HIS PHRASE	באור וחושך—In light and in darkness
HIS BLESSING	He will be a source of strength both in days of joy and darkness.

GEVA גבע

HEBREW	Hill
GEMATRIA	75
HIS WORD	כהן—Priest (Gen. 14:18)
HIS PHRASE	לב גדול—A big heart
HIS BLESSING	Like the priest of old, he will serve God and man with a full heart.

GEYORA גיורא

HEBREW	Shooter
GEMATRIA	220
HIS WORD	רך—Tender (Gen. 18:7)
HIS PHRASE	הלומד מכל אדם—One who learns from all people
HIS BLESSING	Tender and sensitive, he will be wise enough to learn from many different people.

GIBOR גבור

HEBREW	Strong
GEMATRIA	211
HIS WORD	ירא—(God) fearing (Gen. 22:12)
HIS PHRASE	כח גדול ויד חזקה—Great power and a strong hand
HIS BLESSING	His strength and power will be joined in a God-fearing personality.

GIDEON גדעון

HEBREW	Mighty warrior
GEMATRIA	133
HIS WORD	למנחה—For a gift offering (Lev. 7:37)
HIS PHRASE	בחמלה גדולה—With great compassion
HIS BLESSING	He will be generous and compassionate while fighting for what he believes in.

GIL גיל

HEBREW	Joy
GEMATRIA	43
HIS WORD	גדול—Great (Gen. 4:13)
HIS PHRASE	ידי הזהב—Golden hands
HIS BLESSING	A true joy—with hands of gold he cannot fail to succeed.

GILAD גלעד

HEBREW	Hill of testimony
GEMATRIA	107
HIS WORD	נבנה—We will build (Gen. 11:4)
HIS PHRASE	טוב במח ובלב—Good in mind and heart
HIS BLESSING	He will be blessed with intellect as well as sensitivity. He will testify to the value of his faith.

GINSON גנתון

VARIANT	Ginton
HEBREW	Garden, orchard
GEMATRIA	509
HIS WORD	בראשו—With his head (Lev. 5:24)
HIS PHRASE	כשליח מצוה—Like a messenger of *mitzvah* (good deed)
HIS BLESSING	With his mind, he will seek out good deeds to perform. His life will be as fruitful and beautiful as a precious garden.

GITAI גתי

HEBREW	One who presses grapes
GEMATRIA	413
HIS WORD	גשמיכם—Your rains (Lev. 26:4)
HIS PHRASE	בפרי הלולים—With praiseworthy fruits
HIS BLESSING	Whatever he grows will prosper. The fruits of his labors will be many.

GIVON גבעון

HEBREW	Hill
GEMATRIA	131
HIS WORD	והצל—And saved (Ex. 5:23)
HIS PHRASE	האהבה והאמונה—Love and faith
HIS BLESSING	He will rise to great heights and be a savior in the eyes of many.

GOEL גואל

HEBREW	The redeemer
GEMATRIA	40
HIS WORD	חלב—The fat, the best (Gen. 45:18)
HIS PHRASE	לב האב—The heart of his father
HIS BLESSING	He will inherit the best traits of his father. He will help and redeem the low and the troubled.

GOMER גומר

HEBREW	To complete
GEMATRIA	249
HIS WORD	ואברכך—And I will bless you (Gen. 12:2)
HIS PHRASE	החיים לפניו—Life is before him
HIS BLESSING	Life will constantly offer him new challenges to complete and to be blessed. He will be a perfectionist, finishing whatever he starts.

GOREN גורן

HEBREW	Throat
GEMATRIA	259
HIS WORD	המטהר—The one who purifies (Lev. 14:11)
HIS PHRASE	על פי הדין—In accordance with the law
HIS BLESSING	His voice will render judgement and he will be heard.

GOVER גובר

HEBREW	Victorious
GEMATRIA	211
HIS WORD	נבור*—Strong (Gen. 10:9)
HIS PHRASE	אדם עליון—A superior person
HIS BLESSING	He will succeed with strength and be acknowledged as superior.

GURIEL גוריאל

HEBREW	God is my lion
GEMATRIA	250
HIS WORD	נר—Lamp (Ex. 27:20)
HIS PHRASE	אור גדול—Great light
HIS BLESSING	He will be a source of light to others.

GURION גוריון

HEBREW	A young lion
GEMATRIA	275
HIS WORD	רעה—A shepherd (Gen. 4:2)
HIS PHRASE	רוב בינה—An excess of true understanding
HIS BLESSING	With maturity beyond his years, he will be a leader and shepherd among men.

H

HADAR הדר

HEBREW	Adornment, glory, majesty
GEMATRIA	209
HIS WORD	הצדיק—The righteous one (Ex. 9:27)
HIS PHRASE	החכם מכולם—The wisest of all of them
HIS BLESSING	His brilliance will be his chief adornment, gaining him glory and majesty.

HAREL הראל

HEBREW	Mountain of God
GEMATRIA	236
HIS WORD	לדבר—Speak (Gen. 17:22)
HIS PHRASE	רוח טובה—A good spirit
HIS BLESSING	He will ascend to great heights and speak with great eloquence.

HEVEL הבל

HEBREW	Breath, vapor
GEMATRIA	37
HIS WORD	הלב*—The heart (Jeremiah 17:9)
HIS PHRASE	בכבוד אב—With parental honor
HIS BLESSING	With every breath he will express parental devotion with his whole heart.

HILLEL הלל

HEBREW	Praised, famous
GEMATRIA	65
HIS WORD	אדני—My Lord (Gen. 23:6)
HIS PHRASE	כאחד יחיד—Like one alone
HIS BLESSING	He will achieve prominence and praise because of his uniqueness.

HOD הוד

HEBREW	Splendor, vigor
GEMATRIA	15
HIS WORD	אביב—Spring (Ex. 9:31)
HIS PHRASE	או אז—Or then
HIS BLESSING	Ever youthful and vigorous, he will never give up in all of his goals.

HODAYA הודיה

HEBREW	God is my splendor
GEMATRIA	30
HIS WORD	יהודה*—Judah (Gen. 29:35)
HIS PHRASE	ביד זהב—With a golden hand
HIS BLESSING	His grateful spirit and his golden abilities will endear him to others and make him a born leader.

HOSHEA הושע

HEBREW	To help
GEMATRIA	381
HIS WORD	השלום—The peace (Gen. 29:6)
HIS PHRASE	בכח הרצון—With the power of will
HIS BLESSING	Highly motivated and anxious to help others, he will be instrumental in bringing about peace.

I

IDAN עידן

HEBREW	Time
GEMATRIA	134
HIS WORD	חלמנו—That we dreamed (Gen. 40:8)
HIS PHRASE	ליום הגדול—For the great day
HIS BLESSING	He will dream great dreams and will live to achieve them.

IDO אידו

HEBREW	To evaporate
GEMATRIA	21
HIS WORD	אחזה—A possession (Gen. 47:11)
HIS PHRASE	הוא אח—He is a brother
HIS BLESSING	As close as a brother to many, he will possess friends in abundance.

ILAN אילן

HEBREW	Tree
GEMATRIA	91
HIS WORD	מלאך—Angel (Gen. 16:7)
HIS PHRASE	מח גדול—A great mind
HIS BLESSING	He will constantly grow to greater heights with the greatness of his intellect.

IMRI אמרי

HEBREW	My utterance
GEMATRIA	251
HIS WORD	מורה—Teacher (Gen. 12:6)
HIS PHRASE	בחכמה העליונה—With a higher intelligence
HIS BLESSING	He will tower over others in his ability to teach and to communicate.

ITIEL איתיאל

HEBREW	God is with me
GEMATRIA	452
HIS WORD	בתים—Houses (Ex. 1:21)
HIS PHRASE	שמחה גדולה מאד—Very great rejoicing
HIS BLESSING	Family, peace, and happiness will be his as God will always be with him.

ITTAMAR איתמר

HEBREW	Island or palm
GEMATRIA	651
HIS WORD	תרומה—A gift, an offering (Ex. 25:2)
HIS PHRASE	שליח הצבור—Messenger of the community, a cantor
HIS BLESSING	He will ably represent others and be blessed with an extremely generous nature.

IVRI עברי

HEBREW	A Hebrew
GEMATRIA	282
HIS WORD	ברכני—Bless me (Gen. 27:34)
HIS PHRASE	רוח חיים—The spirit of life
HIS BLESSING	In the tradition of Abraham, the first Hebrew, he will be blessed for his courage, individuality, and vibrant spirit.

I Y O V אִיּוֹב

VARIANT	Job
HEBREW	Hated, oppressed
GEMATRIA	19
HIS WORD	ויבא*—And he came (Gen. 7:7)
HIS PHRASE	החג בא—The holiday has come
HIS BLESSING	He will turn every bad moment into a day of rejoicing and feasting.

K

KADMIEL קדמיאל

HEBREW	God is the ancient one
GEMATRIA	185
HIS WORD	הפנים—The face (Ex. 35:13)
HIS PHRASE	ענוה וגדולה—Humility and greatness
HIS BLESSING	With beauty of face and humbleness of character, he will achieve greatness.

KALIL כליל

HEBREW	Crown, wreath
GEMATRIA	90
HIS WORD	מכל—From everything (Gen. 2:2)
HIS PHRASE	מאד מאד—Exceedingly much
HIS BLESSING	He will be crowned with honor and wealth.

KALONYMUS קלונימוס

HEBREW	Merciful
GEMATRIA	302
HIS WORD	בקר—Morning (Gen. 1:5)
HIS PHRASE	עם נדיבי עמו—With the benefactors of his people
HIS BLESSING	He will be enabled to express his gracious and merciful character as a philanthropist amongst his people in the morning of his life.

KANIEL קְנִיאֵל

HEBREW	Reed, stalk
GEMATRIA	191
HIS WORD	הצילנו—Saved us (Ex. 2:19)
HIS PHRASE	אכן מזל גדול—Indeed great good fortune
HIS BLESSING	He will be blessed with great *mazel* (good luck) and be able to help save many people.

KASRIEL כתריאל

VARIANT	Katriel
HEBREW	Crown of the Lord
GEMATRIA	661
HIS WORD	הנרות—The lamps, the candles (Lev. 24:4)
HIS PHRASE	ניצוץ קדושה—A spark of holiness
HIS BLESSING	He will be a light unto others as is a candle in darkness.

KEDEM קֶדֶם

HEBREW	Old, ancient, from the east
GEMATRIA	144
HIS WORD	פדין—Redemption (Ex. 21:30)
HIS PHRASE	באמונה ובלב—With faith and with heart
HIS BLESSING	He will redeem the oppressed with his vision of ideal days of old.

KENAN קֵינָן

HEBREW	To acquire
GEMATRIA	210
HIS WORD	הגבר—The mighty (Deut. 10:17)
HIS PHRASE	חכם ועניו—Wise and humble
HIS BLESSING	He will acquire much through his wisdom, yet retain his humility.

KEREN קֶרֶן

HEBREW	Horn, shone
GEMATRIA	350
HIS WORD	שׂכל—Dealt wisely (Gen. 48:14)
HIS PHRASE	בכבוד ויקר—With honor and glory
HIS BLESSING	He will shine forth with his wisdom and achieve honor and glory.

KESHET קֶשֶׁת

HEBREW	Rainbow, arch
GEMATRIA	800
HIS WORD	תת—Give, yield (Gen. 4:12)
HIS PHRASE	במחשבה תחלה—With prior thought
HIS BLESSING	With much thought, he will give of himself to others and achieve inner peace and harmony.

KITRON כתרון

HEBREW	Crown
GEMATRIA	676
HIS WORD	ולשמש—And to the sun (Deut. 17:3)
HIS PHRASE	מזל רב והצלחה מרובה—Great good fortune and outstanding success
HIS BLESSING	He will be crowned with success and wealth.

KOREN קוֹרֵן

HEBREW	Shining, beaming
GEMATRIA	356
HIS WORD	ויספר—And he told (Gen. 24:66)
HIS PHRASE	הדור מצוה—Beautifying a commandment
HIS BLESSING	He will go out of his way to do everything in a brilliant manner. He will be an excellent conversationalist.

KORESH כורש

VARIANT	Cyrus
HEBREW	Sun
GEMATRIA	526
HIS WORD	רכוש*—Wealth (Gen. 14:11)
HIS PHRASE	מלכי בית דוד—Kings of the house of David
HIS BLESSING	Royal wealth will be his.

L

LAADAN לעדן

HEBREW	For delight
GEMATRIA	154
HIS WORD	ונסלח—And shall be forgiven (Lev. 4:20)
HIS PHRASE	נוהגים בו כבוד—He will be accorded honor
HIS BLESSING	He will bring delight to others and be forgiven his indiscretions.

LAEL לאל

HEBREW	Belonging to God
GEMATRIA	61
HIS WORD	היום—Today (Gen. 1:14)
HIS PHRASE	ילד טוב—A good child
HIS BLESSING	He will be an exceptionally good child making every day special.

LAPIDOS לפידות

VARIANT	Lapidot
HEBREW	Torches
GEMATRIA	530
HIS WORD	שכרי—My reward, my wages (Gen. 30:18)
HIS PHRASE	טובים השנים מהאחד—Two are better than one
HIS BLESSING	He will light the way for others and be a reward to his parents.

LAVAN לבן

VARIANT	Laban
HEBREW	White
GEMATRIA	82
HIS WORD	מלבי—From my heart (Num. 16:28)
HIS PHRASE	בלב חם—With a warm heart
HIS BLESSING	Purity of heart will be his chief characteristic.

LAVI לביא

HEBREW	Lion
GEMATRIA	43
HIS WORD	*לאבי—For my father (Gen. 44:32)
HIS PHRASE	ידי הזהב—Golden hands
HIS BLESSING	With the strength of a lion, he will be a great help to his parents.

LEE לי

HEBREW	To me, mine
GEMATRIA	40
HIS WORD	חלב—The fat, the best (Gen. 45:18)
HIS PHRASE	אהוב ה"—Friend of God
	(ה" is the four letter name of God equaling 26)
HIS BLESSING	He will be the very best friend to many people.

LEOR ליאור

HEBREW	I have light
GEMATRIA	247
HIS WORD	מרבה—Increasing (Lev. 11:42)
HIS PHRASE	כבוד והדר—Honor and glory
HIS BLESSING	His influence on others will increase throughout his life and he will gain ever greater honors.

LESHEM לֶשֶׁם

HEBREW	A precious stone
GEMATRIA	370
HIS WORD	שׁלם*—Whole, complete (Gen. 14:18)
HIS PHRASE	נקי וצדיק—Pure and righteous
HIS BLESSING	He will achieve harmony, wholeness, and completion.

LEV לֵב

HEBREW	Heart
GEMATRIA	32
HIS WORD	כבוד—Glory (Ex. 16:7)
HIS PHRASE	זה ההוד—This is the glory
HIS BLESSING	He will epitomize good-heartedness and feeling, gaining him respect and glory.

LEVI לֵוִי

HEBREW	Joined
GEMATRIA	46
HIS WORD	יודוך—Will praise you (Gen. 49:8)
HIS PHRASE	לב זהב—A golden heart
HIS BLESSING	Joined to others by his golden heart, he will earn praise and plaudits.

LIRON לִירֹן

HEBREW	Song is mine
GEMATRIA	290
HIS WORD	רץ—Ran (Gen. 18:7)
HIS PHRASE	צעד נכון—Proper step
HIS BLESSING	He will speedily achieve his goals and lead a life of song.

LOT לוט

HEBREW	Hidden, covered
GEMATRIA	45
HIS WORD	מאד—Very much (Gen. 1:33)
HIS PHRASE	ידיד טוב—A good friend
HIS BLESSING	He will achieve very much and his few faults will be covered.

LOTAN לוטן

HEBREW	To envelop
GEMATRIA	95
HIS WORD	יפה—Beautiful (Gen. 12:14)
HIS PHRASE	יגל לבך—Your heart will rejoice
HIS BLESSING	He will be beautiful and envelop others with his personality.

M

MACCABEE מכבי

HEBREW	Hammer
GEMATRIA	72
HIS WORD	חסד—Kindness, mercy (Gen. 24:12)
HIS PHRASE	ידו בכל—His hand in everything
HIS BLESSING	He will be involved with countless projects and complete them with forcefulness.

MAGEN מגן

HEBREW	Protection, protector
GEMATRIA	93
HIS WORD	יגיע—Striving, work (Gen. 31:42)
HIS PHRASE	באהבה וחסד—With love and kindness
HIS BLESSING	He will be known as protector, always striving to help others.

MAHIR מהיר

HEBREW	Industrious, excellent, expert
GEMATRIA	255
HIS WORD	מהרי*—Hurry (Gen. 18:6)
HIS PHRASE	טובה וברכה—Goodness and blessing
HIS BLESSING	He will be known for his ability to speedily achieve his goals.

MALACHI מלאכי

HEBREW	My messenger, minister, servant
GEMATRIA	101
HIS WORD	המלאכה—The work (Gen. 33:14)
HIS PHRASE	טוב בכל לב—Good with his whole heart
HIS BLESSING	He will be delegated to achieve important goals.

MAON מעון

HEBREW	Dwelling
GEMATRIA	166
HIS WORD	עליון—Most high (Gen. 14:18)
HIS PHRASE	אין דומה לך—There is none to compare to you
HIS BLESSING	He will dwell on a higher plane than most men, making him incomparable.

MAOR מאור

HEBREW	Brightness
GEMATRIA	247
HIS WORD	יאריכו—They may be lengthened (Deut. 25:15)
HIS PHRASE	צדיק גדול—A great righteous person
HIS BLESSING	He will be blessed with long days as a reward for his goodness.

MARNIN מרנין

HEBREW	One who creates joy, one who sings
GEMATRIA	350
HIS WORD	שכל—Acted wisely (Gen. 48:14)
HIS PHRASE	בכבוד ויקר—With honor and glory
HIS BLESSING	His wisdom will enable him to bring joy to the world.

MAROM מרום

HEBREW	High place, height
GEMATRIA	286
HIS WORD	פרו—Be fruitful (Gen. 1:22)
HIS PHRASE	ברוח סוד—With secret spirit
HIS BLESSING	He will rise to great heights and be fruitful in his efforts.

MASKIL משכיל

HEBREW	Enlightened, educated
GEMATRIA	400
HIS WORD	למשל—For a proverb (Deut. 28:37)
HIS PHRASE	לשון זהב—A golden tongue
HIS BLESSING	He will be eloquent and highly educated.

MATAN מתן

HEBREW	Gift
GEMATRIA	490
HIS WORD	תמים—Whole, perfect (Gen. 6:9)
HIS PHRASE	יש לנו מזל טוב—We have good fortune
HIS BLESSING	He will be a great gift to his family, a source of much *mazal* (good fortune).

MATMON מטמון

HEBREW	Treasure, wealth, riches
GEMATRIA	145
HIS WORD	המלכים—The kings (Gen. 14:17)
HIS PHRASE	מי ידמה לו—Who can compare to him
HIS BLESSING	He will be exceedingly successful and wealthy.

MATOK מתוק

HEBREW	Sweet
GEMATRIA	546
HIS WORD	תקום*—You will arise (Lev. 19:32)
HIS PHRASE	העושה נסים—One who performs miracles
HIS BLESSING	With sweet disposition, he will achieve miraculous results.

MATTISYAHU מתתיהו

VARIANT	Mattathias
HEBREW	Gift of God
GEMATRIA	861
HIS WORD	ונתתה—And you shall give (Ex. 21:23)
	אמיתית—Truthfulness
HIS PHRASE	אוהב את האמת—He loves truth
HIS BLESSING	He will be devoted to truth and be known for his sincerity.

MATZLIACH מצליח

HEBREW	Successful
GEMATRIA	178
HIS WORD	חפץ—Had delight, desired (Gen. 34:19)
HIS PHRASE	זהו בעל חן—He is a master of charm
HIS BLESSING	He will succeed because of his unique charm.

MAZAL TOV מזל טוב

HEBREW	Good luck
GEMATRIA	94
HIS WORD	ויחלם—And he dreamed (Gen. 28:12)
HIS PHRASE	הטוב והמטיב—The good and good for others
HIS BLESSING	His dreams will be blessed with good fortune.

MEGED מגד

HEBREW	Goodness, sweetness, excellence
GEMATRIA	47
HIS WORD	יגדל—Shall be greater (Gen. 38:11)
HIS PHRASE	בוטח בך—Trust in you
HIS BLESSING	His goodness will inspire trust.

MEIR מאיר

VARIANTS	Meyer, Mei'ir
HEBREW	One who brightens or shines
GEMATRIA	251
HIS WORD	יאמר—It will be said (Gen. 10:9)
HIS PHRASE	בחכמה העליונה—With a higher wisdom
HIS BLESSING	It will be said of him that he possesses a higher intuitive wisdom.

MENACHEM מנחם

HEBREW	Comforter
GEMATRIA	138
HIS WORD	בקול—With a voice (Ex. 19:19)
HIS PHRASE	מלא בינה—Filled with understanding
HIS BLESSING	He will know how to say just the right thing, serving as a source of comfort to others.

MENASHEH מנשה

HEBREW	Causing to forget
GEMATRIA	395
HIS WORD	נשמה*—Soul, living thing (Deut. 20:16)
HIS PHRASE	לא חסר כלום—Not lacking anything
HIS BLESSING	He will be blessed with a soul that can forget hurts and never feel lack.

MERON מירון

HEBREW	Troops, soldiers
GEMATRIA	306
HIS WORD	דבש—Honey (Gen. 43:11)
HIS PHRASE	אב הרחמים—Father of mercy
HIS BLESSING	He will temper his combative nature with sweetness and mercy.

MESHULAM משולם

HEBREW	Peaceful
GEMATRIA	416
HIS WORD	באהבתו—With his love (Gen. 29:20)
HIS PHRASE	נוצר סוד—A keeper of secrets
HIS BLESSING	With a peaceful nature, he will always be fully trusted with confidences.

METAV מיטב

HEBREW	The best
GEMATRIA	61
HIS WORD	היום—The day, today (Gen. 1:14)
HIS PHRASE	אז יכבדוהו—Then they will honor him
HIS BLESSING	The day will come when he will be acknowledged and greatly honored.

METHUSELAH מתושלח

HEBREW	Messenger
GEMATRIA	784
HIS WORD	תשלחום*—You shall send them (Num. 5:3)
HIS PHRASE	לכל העוסקים עם הצבור—For all those who occupy themselves with the community
HIS BLESSING	He will be a messenger on behalf of communal causes.

MICHA מיכה

HEBREW	Who is like God
GEMATRIA	75
HIS WORD	כהן—Priest (Gen. 14:18)
HIS PHRASE	לב גדול—Big heart
HIS BLESSING	He will achieve spiritual leadership and be admired for his goodness.

MICHAEL מיכאל

HEBREW	Who is like God
GEMATRIA	101
HIS WORD	אכלכל—Support (Gen. 50:21)
HIS PHRASE	הטיב להם—He did good for them
HIS BLESSING	He will help to support many needy ones.

MORAN מורן

HEBREW	A plant
GEMATRIA	296
HIS WORD	ערכו—His worth (Ex. 40:4)
HIS PHRASE	אור לגוים—A light to the nations
HIS BLESSING	His worth will be recognized by the world at large.

MORDECHAI מרדכי

HEBREW	Warrior
GEMATRIA	274
HIS WORD	ורחמך—And have compassion upon you (Deut. 13:18)
HIS PHRASE	הצלה והצלחה—Saving and succeeding
HIS BLESSING	He will fight for noble causes and succeed.

MOSHE מֹשֶׁה

HEBREW	Salvation, draw out
GEMATRIA	345
HIS WORD	הַשֵּׁם*—The name (God) (Gen. 6:4)
HIS PHRASE	מגלה רזין—Revealer of secrets
HIS BLESSING	He will comprehend the deepest mysteries of life and share his knowledge with others.

N

NAAMAN נעמן

HEBREW	Sweet, beautiful, pleasant, good
GEMATRIA	210
HIS WORD	הגבר—The mighty (Deut. 10:17)
HIS PHRASE	חכם ועניו—Wise and humble
HIS BLESSING	His beauty will be rooted in his wisdom and his modesty.

NACHMAN נחמן

HEBREW	Comforter
GEMATRIA	148
HIS WORD	יצמח—He will sprout (Gen. 2:5)
HIS PHRASE	גדול ליהודים—Great amongst Jews
HIS BLESSING	He will be a source of comfort to his people, growing in stature year after year.

NACHSHON נחשון

HEBREW	Daring person
GEMATRIA	414
HIS WORD	ואהבת—And you shall love (Lev. 19:18)
HIS PHRASE	לשונו החדה—His sharp tongue
HIS BLESSING	With daring and nerve, he will use his sharp tongue to criticize and improve others—but he will do it with love.

NADAV נדב

VARIANT	Nadab
HEBREW	giver
GEMATRIA	56
HIS WORD	וכל—And everything (Gen. 2:1)
HIS PHRASE	הוא יגאל—He will redeem
HIS BLESSING	He will be a philanthropist and very generous with his time and efforts.

NADIV נדיב

HEBREW	Prince, noble
GEMATRIA	66
HIS WORD	והנה—And behold (Gen. 1:31)
	בדין*—With justice
HIS PHRASE	בו ביום—On that very day
HIS BLESSING	He will dispense immediate judgment in noble fashion.

NAFTALI נפתלי

VARIANT	Naphtali
HEBREW	To wrestle
GEMATRIA	570
HIS WORD	לשמר—To guard (Gen. 3:24)
HIS PHRASE	איש גבור חיל—A man of great strength
HIS BLESSING	He will wrestle with evil and fervently guard his principles.

NAGID נגיד

HEBREW	Ruler, prince
GEMATRIA	67
HIS WORD	אוני—My strength (Gen. 35:18)
HIS PHRASE	בכח היחיד—With the power of the individual
HIS BLESSING	Alone and unafraid, he will fight injustice with strength.

NAHIR נהיר

ARAMAIC	Light
GEMATRIA	265
HIS WORD	נאדרי—Glorious (Ex. 15:6)
HIS PHRASE	אור נגה—A brilliant light
HIS BLESSING	Like a beacon of light, he will illuminate the correct path.

NAOR נאור

HEBREW	Enlightened, cultured
GEMATRIA	257
HIS WORD	נורא*—Awesome (Gen. 28:17)
HIS PHRASE	חכם אף נבון—Wise, even brilliant
HIS BLESSING	Highly cultured and educated, he will bring unique insight to his area of specialization.

NATAN נתן

HEBREW	He gave
GEMATRIA	500
HIS WORD	שר—A captain, a ruler (Gen. 21:22)
HIS PHRASE	פרו ורבו—Be fruitful and multiply
HIS BLESSING	He will be a source of great goodness and have a large family.

NATHANIEL נתנאל

VARIANT	Natanel
HEBREW	Gift of God
GEMATRIA	531
HIS WORD	תמצא—You will find (Gen. 31:32)
HIS PHRASE	לעתיד טוב—For a good future
HIS BLESSING	God's gift to him will be to find ever better days in the future.

NAVON נבון

HEBREW	Wise, clever
GEMATRIA	108
HIS WORD	חנן—Has graciously given (Gen. 33:5)
HIS PHRASE	זה במזל טוב—This one with good fortune
HIS BLESSING	Good luck joined with wisdom insure his success.

NECHEMYA נחמיה

HEBREW	God comforts
GEMATRIA	113
HIS WORD	נביאים—Prophets (Num. 11:29)
HIS PHRASE	אדם חכם—A wise man
HIS BLESSING	With prophetic insight, he will bring comfort to others.

NEGEV נגב

HEBREW	South
GEMATRIA	55
HIS WORD	הן—Behold (Gen. 3:22)
HIS PHRASE	בך הכח—In you is might
HIS BLESSING	He will surprise people with his inner strength and fortitude.

NILI נילי

HEBREW	The glory (or eternity) of Israel will not lie
GEMATRIA	100
HIS WORD	על—On, over, above (Gen. 1:2)
HIS PHRASE	אביך ואמך—Your father and your mother
HIS BLESSING	He will be true to his ancestors and to his past.

N I R ניר

HEBREW	A plow, plowed field
GEMATRIA	260
HIS WORD	הגברים—The mighty men (Gen. 6:4)
HIS PHRASE	מהלומד מכל אדם—From those who learn from every person
HIS BLESSING	Like a field that is plowed, he will take the seeds of others' ideas and bring them to fruition.

N I S S A N ניסן

HEBREW	Flight, standard, emblem. Also, the name of first month of Jewish year
GEMATRIA	170
HIS WORD	לעלם—Forever (Gen. 3:22)
HIS PHRASE	בכל יום ויום—Every single day
HIS BLESSING	His emblem will be daily attention to every detail.

N I S S I M נסים

HEBREW	Signs, miracles
GEMATRIA	160
HIS WORD	כסף—Silver, money (Gen. 17:12)
HIS PHRASE	קול דודי—The voice of my beloved
HIS BLESSING	He will be blessed with miraculous measure of wealth and love.

N I T Z A N ניצן

HEBREW	Bud
GEMATRIA	200
HIS WORD	כנפים—Wings (Ex. 25:20)
HIS PHRASE	בכל ימי חייכם—In all the days of your lives
HIS BLESSING	His potential will take time to develop, but eventually he will soar on the wings of success.

NIV ניב

ARABIC AND ARAMAIC	Speech, expression
GEMATRIA	62
HIS WORD	המזבח—The altar (Gen. 13:4)
HIS PHRASE	במח חד—With sharp intellect
HIS BLESSING	He will be extremely eloquent and intelligent.

NOAH נח

HEBREW	Rest, quiet, peace
GEMATRIA	58
HIS WORD	חן*—Grace, favor (Gen. 6:8)
HIS PHRASE	הבוטח *בה"—One who trusts in God
	(ה" stands for the four letter name of God equaling 26)
HIS BLESSING	With complete trust in God, he will find favor in the eyes of all.

NOAM נועם

HEBREW	Sweetness, friendship
GEMATRIA	166
HIS WORD	עליון—Most high (Gen. 14:18)
HIS PHRASE	אין דומה לך—There is no one like you
HIS BLESSING	His sweetness will make him unique and elevated amongst men.

NODA נודע

HEBREW	Famous, well-known
GEMATRIA	130
HIS WORD	עין—Eye (Ex. 21:24)
HIS PHRASE	זה יפה וטוב—This one is beautiful and good
HIS BLESSING	He will be in the public eye and well-known for his beauty and goodness.

NOGA נוגה

HEBREW	Light, bright
GEMATRIA	64
HIS WORD	ידים—Hands (Gen. 34:21)
HIS PHRASE	די לך—Sufficient for you
HIS BLESSING	His deeds will be sufficient, bringing light and joy to others.

NOY נוי

HEBREW	Beauty
GEMATRIA	66
HIS WORD	יוכל—He can (Gen. 13:16)
HIS PHRASE	בו ביום—On that very day
HIS BLESSING	He will never find any task too difficult. He will not hesitate to begin new projects and complete them in the same day.

NUR נור

ARAMAIC	Fire (of the Lord)
GEMATRIA	256
HIS WORD	הארן—The ark (Ex. 25:14)
HIS PHRASE	בן צדיק—Son of a righteous one
HIS BLESSING	With fire and passion, he will pursue the values of his parents.

O

OBEDIAH עובדיה

VARIANT	Obadiah
HEBREW	Servant of God
GEMATRIA	97
HIS WORD	מלאכו—His angel (Gen. 24:7)
HIS PHRASE	טוב לכל—Good for all
HIS BLESSING	As a servant of God he will be known for his kindness.

ODED עודד

HEBREW	Encourage
GEMATRIA	84
HIS WORD	ידע—Knows (Gen. 3:5)
HIS PHRASE	בכל לב—With all his heart
HIS BLESSING	He will be a source of encouragement to others.

OFER עופר

HEBREW	A young deer
GEMATRIA	356
HIS WORD	וישם—And he put (Gen. 2:8)
HIS PHRASE	שביל זהב—Golden mean
HIS BLESSING	He will live by the golden mean and speedily achieve his goals.

OMRI עמרי

ARABIC	To live, to live long, worship
GEMATRIA	320
HIS WORD	לרעך—To your neighbor (Ex. 20:14)
HIS PHRASE	ברוב עם—With a multitude of people
HIS BLESSING	He will be extremely sociable and blessed with length of days.

OREN אורן

HEBREW	Name of a tree
GEMATRIA	257
HIS WORD	נורא*—Awesome (Gen. 28:17)
HIS PHRASE	לחבר טוב—For a good friend
HIS BLESSING	Sturdy and strong in character, he will remain a good friend for life.

OVADYA עובדיה

HEBREW	Servant of God
GEMATRIA	97
HIS WORD	ולאדון—And for a ruler (Gen. 45:8)
HIS PHRASE	טוב לכל—Good to all
HIS BLESSING	He will achieve prominence and rulership because of his unbounded goodness.

OVED עובד

VARIANT	Obed
HEBREW	Worshipper, worker
GEMATRIA	82
HIS WORD	לבן—White, pure (Gen. 30:35)
HIS PHRASE	בלב חם—With a warm heart
HIS BLESSING	He will be a tireless worker and warm friend.

O Z עז

HEBREW	Strength
GEMATRIA	77
HIS WORD	מלוא—Full (Lev. 5:12)
HIS PHRASE	אדם יחיד—A singular person
HIS BLESSING	He will be a strong and firm individualist.

O Z E R עוזר

HEBREW	Helper
GEMATRIA	283
HIS WORD	זכרון—A remembrance, a memorial (Ex. 17:14)
HIS PHRASE	רוח הנבואה—The spirit of prophecy
HIS BLESSING	He will help others with his special prophetic spirit.

O Z N I אזני

HEBREW	My ear
GEMATRIA	68
HIS WORD	חיים—Life (Gen. 2:7)
HIS PHRASE	אל הלב—To the heart
HIS BLESSING	He will be a wonderful listener and will speak directly from the heart.

P

PALTI פלטי

HEBREW	My escape, deliverance
GEMATRIA	129
HIS WORD	נטע—Planted (Num. 24:6)
HIS PHRASE	מלא חן—Filled with charm
HIS BLESSING	His charm will deliver him from all misfortune.

PENINI פניני

HEBREW	Pearl, precious stone
GEMATRIA	200
HIS WORD	פקודי—Officers (Num. 31:14)
HIS PHRASE	בעמור החכמה—With a pillar of wisdom
HIS BLESSING	He will shine as a leader because of his wisdom.

PERETZ פרץ

HEBREW	Burst forth
GEMATRIA	370
HIS WORD	צפר*—Bird (Num. 22:10)
HIS PHRASE	נקי וצדיק—Pure and righteous
HIS BLESSING	He will travel throughout the world and gain a reputation as one truly righteous.

PESACH פסח

HEBREW	To pass, skip over
GEMATRIA	148
HIS WORD	יצמח—Will sprout (Gen. 2:5)
HIS PHRASE	והוא יכלכלך—And he will support you
HIS BLESSING	He will pass from home to home bringing food and sustenance.

PINCHAS פנחס

HEBREW	Mouth of brass, dark complexion
GEMATRIA	198
HIS WORD	צחק—Laughter (Gen. 21:6)
HIS PHRASE	לבעל ההון—As a master of wealth
HIS BLESSING	He will lead a happy life, enjoying great wealth.

R

RAANAN רענן

HEBREW	Fresh, luxuriant, beautiful
GEMATRIA	370
HIS WORD	שלם—Whole, perfect (Gen. 14:18)
HIS PHRASE	אוצר חכמה—A treasure of wisdom
HIS BLESSING	He will delight those who know him with his perfection.

RACHAMIM רחמים

HEBREW	Compassion, understanding, kindness
GEMATRIA	298
HIS WORD	ומברכיך—And he blesses you (Gen. 27:28)
HIS PHRASE	זו רוח נדיבה—This is a giving spirit
HIS BLESSING	He will be extremely kind and giving.

RACHMIEL רחמיאל

HEBREW	Whom God loves
GEMATRIA	289
HIS WORD	בעזרי—Was my help (Ex. 18:4)
HIS PHRASE	בינה וגבורה—Understanding and strength
HIS BLESSING	He will be beloved by God and a source of strength and wisdom to others.

RAM רם

HEBREW	High, lofty
GEMATRIA	240
HIS WORD	ואברכהו—And I blessed him (Gen. 27:33)
HIS PHRASE	דעה צלולה—A clear mind
HIS BLESSING	Clarity of thought elevates him above others.

RANEN רנן

HEBREW	Singing with joy
GEMATRIA	300
HIS WORD	בעבורך—For your sake (Gen. 3:17)
HIS PHRASE	בן אברהם—A descendant of Abraham
HIS BLESSING	Like Abraham of old he will excel in kindness to strangers.

RAPHAEL רפאל

VARIANT	Rafael
HEBREW	God has healed
GEMATRIA	311
HIS WORD	איש—Man (Gen. 2:24)
HIS PHRASE	באופן קבע—In a fixed manner
HIS BLESSING	He will be consistent in his ways and mature in his thinking throughout his days. He will have a talent for healing others both physically and spiritually.

RAVID רביד

HEBREW	Jewelry, ornament
GEMATRIA	216
HIS WORD	דברי*—Word (Num. 11:23)
HIS PHRASE	להצלחה גדולה—For great success
HIS BLESSING	His words will be as jewels, bringing him great success.

RAVIV רביב

HEBREW	Rain, dew
GEMATRIA	214
HIS WORD	ורבו—Multiply (Gen. 1:22)
HIS PHRASE	זמנים טובים—Good times
HIS BLESSING	Like the rains of blessing, he will bring good times to his friends and family.

RECHAVIA רחביה

HEBREW	Breadth
GEMATRIA	225
HIS WORD	הטהור—The pure one (Gen. 8:20)
HIS PHRASE	עין יפה—A good eye
HIS BLESSING	He will be generous and caring, always judging others favorably.

REGEM רגם

ARABIC	A friend
GEMATRIA	243
HIS WORD	גרם*—He caused (Gen. 49:14)
HIS PHRASE	האזרח הטוב—The good citizen
HIS BLESSING	A true friend, he will cause others to do good as well.

RE'UEL רעואל

HEBREW	Friend of God
GEMATRIA	307
HIS WORD	ואש—And fire (Gen. 19:24)
HIS PHRASE	באור צח—With a pure light
HIS BLESSING	He will express his friendship with God in a passionate and fiery manner.

REUVEN ראובן

VARIANT	Reuben
HEBREW	Behold—a son!
GEMATRIA	259
HIS WORD	המטהר—The one who purifies (Lev. 14:11)
HIS PHRASE	מנהיג העולם—Ruler of the world
HIS BLESSING	Leadership will be his forte, helping to purify others.

RIMON רמון

HEBREW	Pomegranate
GEMATRIA	296
HIS WORD	ערכו—His worth (Ex. 40:4)
HIS PHRASE	אור לגוים—A light to the nations
HIS BLESSING	His true worth will extend far beyond his own family and people.

ROM רם

HEBREW	Height
GEMATRIA	240
HIS WORD	יכיר—He will acknowledge, he will recognize (Deut. 21:17)
HIS PHRASE	דעה צלולה—Clear mind
HIS BLESSING	With clarity of thought, he will attain the greatest heights.

RON רן

VARIANT	Ran
HEBREW	To sing, joy, or song
GEMATRIA	250
HIS WORD	נר*—Candle (Ex. 27:20)
HIS PHRASE	אור גדול—Great light
HIS BLESSING	Like a candle, he will bring light as well as great joy to others.

S

SAADYA סעדיה

HEBREW	God's helper
GEMATRIA	149
HIS WORD	והצליח—And he shall prosper (Gen. 24:40)
HIS PHRASE	עם אהבה ואחוה—With love and brotherhood
HIS BLESSING	He will be known as a helper and he will greatly prosper.

SASSON ששון

HEBREW	Joy
GEMATRIA	656
HIS WORD	התרומה—The gift offering (Ex. 25:3)
HIS PHRASE	יבורך ביתו—His home will be blessed
HIS BLESSING	He will find his greatest joy in his home and family.

SEGEL סגל

HEBREW	Treasure
GEMATRIA	93
HIS WORD	יגיע—Striving, work (Gen. 31:42)
HIS PHRASE	זה אחד מיוחד—This one is unique
HIS BLESSING	He will work diligently to achieve his goals and he will be acknowledged as unique amongst others.

SEGEV שׂגב

HEBREW	Glory, majesty, exalted
GEMATRIA	305
HIS WORD	ירצה—Will be acceptable (Lev. 7:18)
HIS PHRASE	כמו הוא אין בכל העם—There is none like him amongst the entire nation
HIS BLESSING	His majesty will be accepted and acknowledged by others.

SHAANAN שׁאנן

HEBREW	Peaceful, secure
GEMATRIA	401
HIS WORD	אנשים—Man of distinction (Gen. 12:20)
HIS PHRASE	רצון הכל—The will of all
HIS BLESSING	He will be included in the highest circles of leadership, fulfilling the will of his people.

SHABTAI שׁבתאי

HEBREW	Born on Shabbat, rest
GEMATRIA	713
HIS WORD	תשׂיג—You will reach (Lev. 14:30)
HIS PHRASE	בריאות הגוף—Bodily health
HIS BLESSING	He will attain length of days in good health.

SHACHANYAH שׁכניה

HEBREW	Close to God
GEMATRIA	385
HIS WORD	הרקיע—The firmament (Gen. 1:7)
HIS PHRASE	חכמה ומוסר—Wisdom and discipline
HIS BLESSING	He will teach, inspire, and discipline others.

SHAI שַׁי

HEBREW	Gift, present
GEMATRIA	310
HIS WORD	יֵשׁ*—There is, there are (Gen. 18:24)
HIS PHRASE	מזל וברכה—Good luck and blessing
HIS BLESSING	He will be honest and real, a gift to his parents and his community, bringing good luck and blessing.

SHALMAN שַׁלְמָן

HEBREW	To be complete or rewarded
GEMATRIA	420
HIS WORD	לשמן*—For oil (Ex. 25:6)
HIS PHRASE	חיים של טובה—A life of goodness
HIS BLESSING	He will be rewarded for his goodness with a life filled with blessing.

SHALOM שָׁלוֹם

HEBREW	Peace
GEMATRIA	376
HIS WORD	ומשֵׁל*—Ruler (Gen. 45:8)
HIS PHRASE	קוֹל רם—Elevated voice
HIS BLESSING	He will bring peace to others with his powerful voice.

SHAMA שָׁמַע

HEBREW	He heard
GEMATRIA	410
HIS WORD	משכן—Tabernacle (Ex. 38:21)
HIS PHRASE	איש ידיעה—A man of knowledge
HIS BLESSING	He will be an excellent listener, which will grant him more wisdom.

SHAMAI שמאי

HEBREW	Name
GEMATRIA	351
HIS WORD	מאיש*—Out of man (Gen. 2:23)
HIS PHRASE	חבר נאמן—A trustworthy friend
HIS BLESSING	He will be an outstanding friend who will answer whenever called by name.

SHAMIR שמיר

HEBREW	A very strong, rocklike substance
GEMATRIA	550
HIS WORD	שמרי*—Guardian (Num. 3:28)
HIS PHRASE	ראש הגולה—Head of the exile
HIS BLESSING	His strength and his power will help him guard and protect his people.

SHAPIR שפיר

ARAMAIC	Beautiful
GEMATRIA	590
HIS WORD	פרשי*—Spreading out (Ex. 25:20)
HIS PHRASE	שכר הליכה—Reward for going
HIS BLESSING	He will spread out his efforts in many directions, traveling far to achieve his goals.

SHAUL שאול

HEBREW	Asked, borrowed
GEMATRIA	337
HIS WORD	לשוא*—In vain (Ex. 20:7)
HIS PHRASE	עוצו עצה—Seek advice
HIS BLESSING	He will be asked his opinion on many matters and people will borrow from his ideas.

SHAYS שֵׁת

VARIANT	Seth
HEBREW	Garment, appointed
SYRIAN	Appearance
GEMATRIA	700
HIS WORD	כפרת—An ark cover (Ex. 25:17)
HIS PHRASE	שירים יפים—Beautiful songs
HIS BLESSING	He will beautify his surroundings and be known for his song.

SHEFER שֶׁפֶר

HEBREW	Pleasant, beautiful
GEMATRIA	580
HIS WORD	פרש*—Declared, explained (Num. 15:34)
HIS PHRASE	טובים השנים מן האחד—Two are better than one
HIS BLESSING	He will have the ability to explain things in a convincing and beautiful manner. Others will assist him in his tasks.

SHEMAYAHU שמעיהו

ARAMAIC AND HEBREW	God has heard
GEMATRIA	431
HIS WORD	תיטיב—You do well (Gen. 4:7)
HIS PHRASE	חן ושכל טוב—Grace and good sense
HIS BLESSING	His name will be known far and wide for his good sense. He will use his charm well and to his advantage.

SHERAGA שרגא

ARAMAIC	Light
GEMATRIA	504
HIS WORD	לדעת—To know (Gen. 3:22)
HIS PHRASE	בוחן לבות—Probing hearts
HIS BLESSING	He will have intuitive insight into others and be able to shed light on their psychological problems.

SHERIRA שרירא

ARAMAIC	Strong
GEMATRIA	711
HIS WORD	והפריתי—And I will make fruitful (Gen. 17:20)
HIS PHRASE	ככוכבי השמים לרוב—Like the stars of the heavens for multitude
HIS BLESSING	He will be extremely fruitful in numbers of descendants as well as in good deeds.

SHEVACH שבח

HEBREW	Praise
GEMATRIA	310
HIS WORD	חשב*—Skillful workmen, thought (Ex. 26:1)
HIS PHRASE	מזל וברכה—Good luck and blessing
HIS BLESSING	He will be blessed with the ability to think deeply and he will be praised for his profundity.

SHEVNA שבנא

HEBREW	Tender, youth
GEMATRIA	353
HIS WORD	נגש—He drew near (Gen. 33:7)
HIS PHRASE	הוא יאריך ימים—He will have length of days
HIS BLESSING	He will be blessed with a youthful appearance, vigor and long life.

SHIMON שמעון

HEBREW	To be heard, acceptance
GEMATRIA	466
HIS WORD	ויתן—And he gave (Gen. 1:7)
HIS PHRASE	כי לשון זהב לו—For he has a golden tongue
HIS BLESSING	He will be an outstanding speaker and listener. His advice will usually be accepted.

SHIMSHON שמשון

HEBREW	Like the sun
GEMATRIA	696
HIS WORD	ויפתר—And he interpreted, solved (Gen. 41:12)
HIS PHRASE	לדבר בנחת—To speak with calmness (patience)
HIS BLESSING	With the illumination of the sun, he will solve the deepest mysteries.

SHLOMOH שלמה

HEBREW	Peace
GEMATRIA	375
HIS WORD	*המשל—Who rules (Gen. 24:2)
HIS PHRASE	ממלך מלכי המלכים—From the king, king of kings
HIS BLESSING	He will be a leader of men with divinely granted abilities.

SHLUMIEIL שלומיאל

HEBREW	At peace with God
GEMATRIA	417
HIS WORD	וחגו—You will celebrate (Lev. 23:39)
HIS PHRASE	יום הכפורים—The Day of Atonement (Yom Kippur)
HIS BLESSING	He will find total peace, contentment, and forgiveness.

SHMARYAHU שמריהו

HEBREW	God watches
GEMATRIA	561
HIS WORD	נפלאות—Marvels (Ex. 34:10)
HIS PHRASE	גמילות חסד—Acts of loving kindness
HIS BLESSING	He will enjoy special divine protection because of his benevolence.

SHMAYAH שמעיה

HEBREW	God hears
GEMATRIA	425
HIS WORD	השלמים—The peace offering (Lev. 3:3)
HIS PHRASE	אזרח וגר—Native and stranger
HIS BLESSING	His sacrifices, on behalf of friends and strangers, will be heard by God and rewarded.

SHMUEL שמואל

VARIANT	Samuel
HEBREW	God hears
GEMATRIA	377
HIS WORD	ולמשא*—And for bearing burdens
HIS PHRASE	שהכל בך—For everything is in you
HIS BLESSING	He will carry the burdens of all and God will respond to his requests.

SHNEIOR שניאור

HEBREW	Two lights
GEMATRIA	567
HIS WORD	אשרוני*—Will call me happy (Gen. 30:13)
HIS PHRASE	איש דברים—A man of words
HIS BLESSING	His words will bring happiness and enlightenment to others.

SHOAM שוהם

HEBREW	Onyx
GEMATRIA	351
HIS WORD	ושמה*—And there (Gen. 49:31)
HIS PHRASE	חבר נאמן—A faithful friend
HIS BLESSING	People will point him out and say, "There is a paradigm of a true friend."

SHUSHAN שׁוּשַׁן

HEBREW	Flower, lily
GEMATRIA	656
HIS WORD	שָׂשׂוֹן*—Rejoicing (Is. 22:13)
HIS PHRASE	יבורך ביתו—His house will be blessed
HIS BLESSING	His home will be filled with beauty, song, and happiness.

SIMCHA שִׂמְחָה

HEBREW	Joy
GEMATRIA	353
HIS WORD	בארצכם—In your land (Lev. 19:33)
HIS PHRASE	בין אדם לחברו—Between man and his neighbor
HIS BLESSING	He will find happiness on earth because of his ability to relate well to others.

SINAI סִינַי

HEBREW	Clay desert
GEMATRIA	130
HIS WORD	עין—Eye (Ex. 21:26)
HIS PHRASE	זה יפה וטוב—This is beautiful and good
HIS BLESSING	With his discerning eye for improvement, he will have the gift of turning a barren desert into a productive and fruitful place.

SISI שִׂישִׂי

HEBREW	My joy
GEMATRIA	620
HIS WORD	וטהרת—And you shall purify (Num. 8:6)
HIS PHRASE	בצרכי הצבור—In the needs of the community
HIS BLESSING	He will be a community-minded person inspiring others to do good and bringing joy in his wake.

SIVAN סיון

HEBREW	Ninth month after Jewish New Year
GEMATRIA	126
HIS WORD	נכון—Prepared, ready (Gen. 41:32)
HIS PHRASE	ביום מיוחד—On a special day
HIS BLESSING	He will be a master at finding the right moment and the special day to achieve his goals.

T

TABBAI טבאי

ARAMAIC	Good
GEMATRIA	22
HIS WORD	הטוב—What is good (Gen. 16:6)
HIS PHRASE	אב האהוב—Beloved father
HIS BLESSING	He will be an outstanding parent and a very kind person.

TAL טל

HEBREW	Dew, rain
GEMATRIA	39
HIS WORD	הגאל—The redeemer (Gen. 48:16)
HIS PHRASE	זווג טוב—A good partner
HIS BLESSING	He will make an excellent husband and be a good provider.

TALIA טליא

ARAMAIC	A young lamb
GEMATRIA	50
HIS WORD	כל—Everything (Gen. 1:21)
HIS PHRASE	אב ואם—Father and mother
HIS BLESSING	He will incorporate the best of both of his parents.

TALMAI תלמי

HEBREW	Furrow, a mound
GEMATRIA	480
HIS WORD	לנשק—To kiss (Gen. 31:28)
HIS PHRASE	אהבת חסד—Love of kindness
HIS BLESSING	He will rise above and enjoy the highest form of reciprocal love.

TALOR טלאור

HEBREW	Dew of the morning
GEMATRIA	246
HIS WORD	להאיר—To give light (Gen. 1:15)
HIS PHRASE	ברי לבב—Pure of heart
HIS BLESSING	He will give of his blessings to others daily with the goodness and purity of his heart.

TAMIR תמיר

HEBREW	Tall and stately like the palm tree
GEMATRIA	650
HIS WORD	קרשים—Boards (of the sanctuary) (Ex. 26:22)
HIS PHRASE	קדוש ברוך הוא—The Holy One, Blessed Be He
HIS BLESSING	He will protect the values and ideals of the House of God with dignity and strength.

TANCHUM תנחום

HEBREW	Comfort
GEMATRIA	504
HIS WORD	לדעת—To know (Gen 3:22)
HIS PHRASE	לשון חכמים—The language of the wise
HIS BLESSING	He will know how to speak to the hearts of people and how to offer them comfort.

TARPHON טרפון

HEBREW	Gatherer of leaves
GEMATRIA	345
HIS WORD	השם—Name (of God) (Gen. 6:4)
HIS PHRASE	היה לו הרבה מזל—He had a great deal of good fortune
HIS BLESSING	He will be honored with many blessings because of his extra measure of *mazel*.

TEMAN תימן

HEBREW	Right side
GEMATRIA	500
HIS WORD	נתן—Giving (Gen. 24:52)
HIS PHRASE	חכמת לב—Wisdom of the heart
HIS BLESSING	With his intuitive wisdom, he will give good advice to others.

TE'OM (THOMAS) תאום

ARAMAIC AND HEBREW	A twin
GEMATRIA	447
HIS WORD	ואמת*—Truth (Gen. 24:49)
HIS PHRASE	בלי עין הרע—Without the evil eye
HIS BLESSING	He will be doubly blessed. Because of his total dedication to truth, he will not be affected by the envy of others.

TIBON טבעון

HEBREW	Naturalist, student of nature
GEMATRIA	137
HIS WORD	מצבה—A pillar, a monument (Gen. 28:18)
HIS PHRASE	בחוזק יד—With a strong hand
HIS BLESSING	He will have a keen love of nature. With a strong hand he will help to protect the environment.

TOMER תומר

HEBREW	Palm tree
GEMATRIA	646
HIS WORD	וחרם*—And it was lifted up (Gen. 7:17)
HIS PHRASE	לראש העם—To the head of the nation
HIS BLESSING	Standing tall like a palm tree, he will be looked up to by others and he will be appointed to positions of leadership.

TUVYA טוביה

VARIANT	Tuvyah
HEBREW	God's goodness
GEMATRIA	32
HIS WORD	לב—Heart (Gen. 8:21)
HIS PHRASE	אבי אביו—His father's father
HIS BLESSING	He will be like his grandfather, epitomizing the goodness of the Almighty.

TZADOK צדוק

HEBREW	Just
GEMATRIA	200
HIS WORD	פקודי—Officers (Num. 31:14)
HIS PHRASE	והוא חכם ונבון—And he is wise and understanding
HIS BLESSING	He will be a just leader, respected for his intelligence and deep level of understanding.

TZEFANYAH צפניה

HEBREW	Treasured by God
GEMATRIA	235
HIS WORD	הכיר—He recognized (Deut. 33:9)
HIS PHRASE	ברכה בו—Blessing is in him
HIS BLESSING	He will be highly treasured by God and be extremely insightful into other people's true character and nature.

TZEMACH צמח

HEBREW	Sprout
GEMATRIA	138
HIS WORD	מצח*—Forehead (Ex. 28:38)
HIS PHRASE	דיצה וחדוה—Gladness and rejoicing
HIS BLESSING	He will clearly demonstrate to all his good humor and joy in living.

TZEVI צבי

VARIANT	Tzvi
HEBREW	Lord, ruler
GEMATRIA	102
HIS WORD	נחמד—Pleasant (Gen. 2:9)
HIS PHRASE	חיים בכבוד—Life with honor
HIS BLESSING	He will command the respect of many and lead a life of pleasantness and honor.

TZIDKIYAHU צדקיהו

HEBREW	God's justice
GEMATRIA	215
HIS WORD	גביר—Lord, ruler (Gen. 27:29)
HIS PHRASE	דיין נאמן—A just judge
HIS BLESSING	He will be known for his fairness in judgment and be appointed to positions of leadership.

TZION ציון

HEBREW	Excellent, a sign
GEMATRIA	156
HIS WORD	צוני*—Commanded me (Deut. 4:5)
HIS PHRASE	מהולל מאד—Greatly praised
HIS BLESSING	He will be extremely disciplined and orderly and he will be blessed with a sunny disposition.

TZURIEL צוריאל

HEBREW	God is my rock
GEMATRIA	337
HIS WORD	ונרפא—And it is healed (Lev. 13:18)
HIS PHRASE	ולא ייעף ולא ייגע—And he will neither tire nor become weary
HIS BLESSING	He will be blessed with boundless energy and have the power to heal.

U

URI אורי

HEBREW	Light
GEMATRIA	217
HIS WORD	יראו*—They will see (Gen. 12:12)
HIS PHRASE	לך מחיל אל חיל—Go from strength to strength
HIS BLESSING	His life will be a progression from year to year of great growth, productivity, and blessing, which will be readily seen by all.

URIEL אוריאל

HEBREW	God is my flame
GEMATRIA	248
HIS WORD	וברכך—And bless you (Deut. 7:13)
HIS PHRASE	חפץ בחיים—Desiring life
HIS BLESSING	His passion for life and joy for living will bring him much blessing.

UZI עוזי

HEBREW	My strength
GEMATRIA	93
HIS WORD	מגן—Shield (Gen. 15:1)
HIS PHRASE	מגדל גבוה—A high tower
HIS BLESSING	He will, with his strength of character, protect and defend his family and loved ones.

UZZIEL עוזיאל

HEBREW	Power of God
GEMATRIA	124
HIS WORD	עדן—Eden (garden of) (Gen. 2:15)
HIS PHRASE	הוא חביב מכל—He is dearest of all
HIS BLESSING	He will be the most beloved of all. The power he possesses will turn his surroundings into a paradise.

V

VERED ורד

HEBREW	The rose
GEMATRIA	210
HIS WORD	רדו*—Descend (Gen. 42:2)
HIS PHRASE	חכם ועניו—Wise and humble
HIS BLESSING	He will be able to lower himself from his lofty peak to bring beauty and love into the lives of others.

Y

YAAKOV יעקב

VARIANT	Yakov
HEBREW	Supplanter, held by the heel
GEMATRIA	182
HIS WORD	בעינים—With eyes, at "Enayim" (a place) (Gen. 38:21)
HIS PHRASE	בין אדם לאדם—Between man and man
HIS BLESSING	He will see eye to eye with others and be adept at interpersonal relationships.

YAAR יער

HEBREW	Forest
GEMATRIA	280
HIS WORD	עיר*—City (Gen. 4:17)
HIS PHRASE	אור החיים—The light of life
HIS BLESSING	He will be drawn to both the rural and rustic, finding much joy in each of them.

YADIN ידין

HEBREW	He will judge
GEMATRIA	74
HIS WORD	וחכם—And wise (Gen. 41:33)
HIS PHRASE	ידי זהב לו—He has golden hands
HIS BLESSING	He will be an artisan and an able craftsman. He will know how to properly judge and evaluate people and ideas.

YAGEL יגל

HEBREW	To reveal, to uncover
GEMATRIA	43
HIS WORD	גדול—Great (Gen. 4:13)
HIS PHRASE	בכח אהבה—With the power of love
HIS BLESSING	He will plumb secrets that others cannot fathom. With the power of his love, he will have many open their hearts to him.

YAGIL יגיל

HEBREW	To rejoice
GEMATRIA	53
HIS WORD	החיל—The wealth (Deut. 8:17)
HIS PHRASE	החוזה הטוב—The good seer
HIS BLESSING	He will have a pleasant disposition and a happy demeanor. He will see only the good in others.

YAIR יאיר

HEBREW	He will enlighten
GEMATRIA	221
HIS WORD	יראי*—(God) fearing (Ex. 18:21)
HIS PHRASE	בגדולי עמנו—Amongst the great of our nation
HIS BLESSING	He will achieve greatness and enlighten others with his wisdom and spirituality.

YAKIR יקיר

HEBREW	Dear, beloved, honorable
GEMATRIA	320
HIS WORD	לרעך—To your neighbor (Ex. 20:14)
HIS PHRASE	נקיי כפים—Those with clean hands
HIS BLESSING	He will be totally honest and beyond reproach. He will be beloved by friends and neighbors for his scrupulous behavior.

YARDAN ירדן

VARIANT	Jordan
HEBREW	Descending
GEMATRIA	264
HIS WORD	רחמיו—His mercy (Gen. 43:30)
HIS PHRASE	אדם טוב ומנומס—A good and sensitive man
HIS BLESSING	He will not hesitate to humble himself and to be merciful to others. His sensitive and refined nature will make an impression on people.

YARKON ירקון

HEBREW	Green
GEMATRIA	366
HIS WORD	ונחשב—And be reckoned, be counted (Num. 18:27)
HIS PHRASE	אומר מעט—Saying little
HIS BLESSING	With few words he will accomplish much. His will and desires will quickly be turned into action.

YARON ירון

VARIANT	Jaron
HEBREW	He will cry out, he will sing
GEMATRIA	266
HIS WORD	מכור—Out of the furnace (Deut. 4:20)
HIS PHRASE	הוא רחום—He will have mercy
HIS BLESSING	A compassionate and caring soul, he will take pity on all those who cry out, helping them in time of their affliction.

YAVNIEL יבניאל

HEBREW	God will build
GEMATRIA	103
HIS WORD	הכוכבים—Stars (Gen. 1:16)
HIS PHRASE	אני אבטח בך—I trust in you
HIS BLESSING	He will reach for the stars as he builds and creates. He will inspire the trust of others.

YECHEZKIEL יחזקאל

HEBREW	Might of God
GEMATRIA	156
HIS WORD	עוֹף—Bird (Gen. 1:21)
HIS PHRASE	לחן ולכבוד—For grace and for glory
HIS BLESSING	His ideas will soar and he will be greatly honored.

YECHIEL יחיאל

HEBREW	May God live
GEMATRIA	59
HIS WORD	אחים—Brothers (Gen. 13:8)
HIS PHRASE	הלב הטוב—The good heart
HIS BLESSING	His goodness will acquaint him with many friends who will be as dear to him as brothers.

YEDID ידיד

HEBREW	Beloved, friend
GEMATRIA	28
HIS WORD	כח—Power, might (Num. 14:17)
HIS PHRASE	די בזה—Sufficient with this one
HIS BLESSING	He will be a true friend who will sufficiently fulfill the needs of others.

YEDIEL ידיאל

HEBREW	Knowing the Lord
GEMATRIA	55
HIS WORD	הן—Behold (Gen. 3:22)
HIS PHRASE	הוא גדול—He is great
HIS BLESSING	He will intuitively know a great deal and will always surprise others with his creativity.

YEFES יפת

VARIANT	Yefet
HEBREW	Handsome
GEMATRIA	490
HIS WORD	תמלך—You will reign (Gen. 37:8)
HIS PHRASE	מדור לדור—From generation to generation
HIS BLESSING	With his beautiful appearance he will lead and rule, uniting generations both past and future.

YEHOASH יהואש

HEBREW	God gave
GEMATRIA	322
HIS WORD	והאיש*—And the man (Gen. 24:21)
HIS PHRASE	יצר הטוב—The good inclination
HIS BLESSING	He will be mature beyond his years and follow his basic inclination for goodness.

YEHONADAV יהונדב

HEBREW	God gives
GEMATRIA	77
HIS WORD	עז—Strength, power (Gen. 49:3)
HIS PHRASE	אדם יחיד—A singular person
HIS BLESSING	His strength of character and fortitude will make him unique among men.

YEHONASAN יהונתן

VARIANT	Yehonatan
HEBREW	Gift of God
GEMATRIA	521
HIS WORD	ראשך—Your head (Gen. 40:19)
HIS PHRASE	אין כמעשיך—There is none like your deeds
HIS BLESSING	His intellect will guide his actions. His deeds and achievements will stand out from the crowd.

YEHOSHUA יְהוֹשֻׁעַ

VARIANT	Joshua
HEBREW	God's help
GEMATRIA	391
HIS WORD	ויעשה*—And he offered it (Lev. 9:16)
HIS PHRASE	ולעיני כל העמים—And in the sight of all the nations
HIS BLESSING	God will help him to achieve universal recognition.

YEHOYAKIM יְהוֹיָקִים

VARIANT	Jehoyakim
HEBREW	God will establish
GEMATRIA	181
HIS WORD	מאסף—Gatherer (Num. 10:25)
HIS PHRASE	נביא הנביאים—A prophet of prophets
HIS BLESSING	Gifted with almost divine insight, he will be able to establish unity between dissidents.

YEHUDAH יְהוּדָה

HEBREW	Praise
GEMATRIA	30
HIS WORD	יהיה—He will be (Gen. 1:29)
HIS PHRASE	ביד זהב—With golden hand
HIS BLESSING	He will be all that he can be and others greatly praise his accomplishments.

YEHUDI יְהוּדִי

HEBREW	Jew
GEMATRIA	35
HIS WORD	אלד—I will give birth (Gen. 18:13)
HIS PHRASE	אבי הטוב—My good father
HIS BLESSING	He will give birth to descendants who will bring pride and joy to his parents.

YEKUTIEL יקותיאל

HEBREW	One who harkens to the Lord, to understand
GEMATRIA	557
HIS WORD	ראשון—The first, the chief (Ex. 12:2)
HIS PHRASE	ראוי לשבח—Praiseworthy
HIS BLESSING	He will be a leader worthy of praise and respect.

YERACHMIEL ירחמיאל

HEBREW	Whom God loves
GEMATRIA	299
HIS WORD	בעזרך—With your help (Deut. 33:26)
HIS PHRASE	אדם רך לבב—A person of tender heart
HIS BLESSING	His tender spirit and sensitivity will make him much beloved. He will always seek the help of others.

YERUCHAM ירוחם

HEBREW	Loved, finding mercy
GEMATRIA	264
HIS WORD	רחמיו*—His mercy (Gen. 43:30)
HIS PHRASE	חן עצום—Outstanding charm
HIS BLESSING	His merciful nature with his charismatic charm will bring him many friends and admirers.

YESHAYAHU ישעיהו

VARIANT	Yeshaiyahu
HEBREW	God lends
GEMATRIA	401
HIS WORD	נשיאם—Princes (Gen. 17:20)
HIS PHRASE	שליט בכל—Ruling over all
HIS BLESSING	With his dominating personality he will rule over others and be a born leader.

YESHURUN יְשׁוּרוּן

HEBREW	Upright, honest
GEMATRIA	572
HIS WORD	וְיִרַשְׁנוּ*—And we will inherit (Num. 13:30)
HIS PHRASE	מִי שֶׁבֵּרַךְ—The one who blessed
HIS BLESSING	He will inherit the best qualities of his parents and ancestors. While possessing the ability to bless others, he will have his blessings fulfilled.

YIFTOCH יִפְתַּח

HEBREW	Will open
GEMATRIA	498
HIS WORD	מִנְחָה—Meal offering (Lev. 2:7)
HIS PHRASE	יוֹם צוֹם כִּפּוּר—The day of the Fast of Atonement
HIS BLESSING	He will open the hearts of many to the ideals of gratitude and atonement.

YIGAL יִגְאָל

HEBREW	He will redeem
GEMATRIA	44
HIS WORD	וְגִלָּה—And he will reveal (Lev. 20:18)
HIS PHRASE	וּבְכֹחַ הָאָב—And with the father's power
HIS BLESSING	With the powers of past generations he will reveal truths previously hidden and this will help to redeem his people.

YIRMIYAHU יִרְמִיָהוּ

HEBREW	God appointed
GEMATRIA	271
HIS WORD	לְמָאֹר—To give light (Ex. 25:6)
HIS PHRASE	הֵאָסְפוּ וְאַגִּידָה לָכֶם—Gather together and I will reveal to you
HIS BLESSING	He will be divinely appointed to reveal spiritual light and truths.

YISHAI יִשַׁי

HEBREW	Wealthy, gift
GEMATRIA	320
HIS WORD	לרעך—To your neighbor (Ex. 20:14)
HIS PHRASE	ככלי כסף וכלי זהב—Like vessels of silver and gold
HIS BLESSING	He will be exceedingly wealthy and he will share his good fortune with his neighbors.

YISHMAEL יִשְׁמָעֵאל

VARIANT	Ishmael
HEBREW	God will hear
GEMATRIA	451
HIS WORD	תהום—The depths (Gen. 1:2)
HIS PHRASE	אמונה של איוב—The faith of Job
HIS BLESSING	No matter his difficulties, he will maintain an optimistic belief in divine providence.

YISRAEL יִשְׂרָאֵל

HEBREW	Prince of God, strove with God
GEMATRIA	541
HIS WORD	והצלתי—And I will save (Ex. 6:6)
HIS PHRASE	דרך חדשה—A new way
HIS BLESSING	He will be a great innovator, fighting bravely for his beliefs.

YISSACHAR יִשָׂשׂכָר

HEBREW	There is a reward
GEMATRIA	830
HIS WORD	לתת—To give (Gen. 15:7)
HIS PHRASE	במזל ובברכה לכל המשפחה—With good fortune and blessing to the entire family
HIS BLESSING	He will be doubly rewarded for his goodness—both for himself and his loved ones.

YITZCHAK יצחק

HEBREW	He will laugh
GEMATRIA	208
HIS WORD	ארבה—I will increase (Gen. 3:16)
HIS PHRASE	מכלכל חיים—Sustains life
HIS BLESSING	He will help to support others, bringing laughter and joy to his surroundings.

YOAV יואב

HEBREW	God is my father
GEMATRIA	19
HIS WORD	ואבי*—And the father of (Gen. 11:29)
HIS PHRASE	החג בא—The festival comes
HIS BLESSING	He will have a strong attachment to his parents. He will be as treasured as a festival.

YOEL יואל

HEBREW	God is willing
GEMATRIA	47
HIS WORD	אליו*—To him (Gen. 8:9)
HIS PHRASE	בטחו בך—They trust in you
HIS BLESSING	He will be exceedingly trustworthy. People will turn to him for advice and counsel.

YOHANAN יוחנן

HEBREW	The Lord graced
GEMATRIA	124
HIS WORD	עדן—Eden (garden of) (Gen. 2:15)
HIS PHRASE	יום מיוחד—A special day
HIS BLESSING	His birthday will be celebrated as a special day of God's grace. He will bring a flavor of paradise to his parents.

YOM TOV יום טוב

HEBREW	Holiday
GEMATRIA	73
HIS WORD	חכמה—Wisdom (Ex. 28:3)
HIS PHRASE	זה היום—Today
HIS BLESSING	He will never delay what must be done. Every day will be turned into a meaningful moment by his wisdom.

YONAH יונה

HEBREW	Dove
GEMATRIA	71
HIS WORD	מלא—Full (Gen. 23:9)
HIS PHRASE	כח גדול—Great power
HIS BLESSING	He will use his strength to bring about peace.

YONATAN יונתן

HEBREW	Gift of God
GEMATRIA	516
HIS WORD	יתננו*—He shall give it (Lev. 5:24)
HIS PHRASE	רבים רחמיו—Great are his mercies
HIS BLESSING	His chief delight will be in sharing the gifts he has received from God with others less fortunate.

YORA יורה

HEBREW	To teach
GEMATRIA	221
HIS WORD	הורי*—My parents, my ancestors (Gen. 49:26)
HIS PHRASE	נאמן לכל—Faithful to all
HIS BLESSING	He will show others what his parents have taught him. He will be trusted and loved by all.

YORAM יורם

HEBREW	God is exalted
GEMATRIA	256
HIS WORD	הארן—The ark (Ex. 25:14)
HIS PHRASE	נאה מקיים—One who fulfills his words well
HIS BLESSING	He will be true to his inner convictions. Whatever he commits himself to do, he will fulfill.

YORON יורן

HEBREW	Singing
GEMATRIA	266
HIS WORD	מבחריו—From his youth (Num. 11:28)
HIS PHRASE	הוא רחום—He is merciful
HIS BLESSING	In his early years he will exhibit special traits of mercy and compassion. He will carry out his good deeds with joy and song.

YOSEF יוסף

HEBREW	God will increase
GEMATRIA	156
HIS WORD	ויסף—And he added, increased (Gen. 8:10)
HIS PHRASE	מהולל מאד—Highly praised
HIS BLESSING	He will bring together those who are estranged and he will gather much riches.

YOSHIYAH יושיה

HEBREW	God's help
GEMATRIA	331
HIS WORD	נרפא—Was healed (Lev. 13:37)
HIS PHRASE	לא ייעף ולא יינע—He will neither tire nor weary
HIS BLESSING	He will be a born helper and healer, exhibiting boundless energy.

YOTAM יותם

VARIANT	Jotham
HEBREW	God is perfect
GEMATRIA	456
HIS WORD	תוכל—You will be able (Gen. 15:5)
HIS PHRASE	לך לשלום—Go in peace
HIS BLESSING	Nothing will ever be too difficult for him—he will find peace and perfection.

YOVIN יבין

HEBREW	He will understand
GEMATRIA	72
HIS WORD	חסד—Kindness, mercy (Gen. 24:12)
HIS PHRASE	ידו בכל—His hand is in everything
HIS BLESSING	He will understand how to be involved in numerous projects at the same time. He will be known for his energy, commitment, and kindness.

YUDAN יודן

HEBREW	To judge, to be judged
GEMATRIA	70
HIS WORD	ידון*—Strive (Gen. 6:3)
HIS PHRASE	אבי ואמי—My father and my mother
HIS BLESSING	He will bring the compassion of a mother and the discipline of a father to his judgments. He will be respected as a communal judge and leader.

YUVAL יובל

HEBREW	River, stream
GEMATRIA	48
HIS WORD	הגדול—The great one (Gen. 10:21)
HIS PHRASE	בכח האהבה—With the power of love
HIS BLESSING	Like a rushing stream, his love will flow, encompassing many in distant places.

Z

ZABDI זַבְדִּי

HEBREW	Gift
GEMATRIA	23
HIS WORD	וטוב—And good (Gen. 2:9)
HIS PHRASE	אח אהוב—A beloved brother
HIS BLESSING	He will bring unto others the gift of great friendship. He will be like a brother to countless people.

ZAKKAI זַכַּאי

HEBREW	Pure, clean, innocent
GEMATRIA	38
HIS WORD	לבו—His heart (Gen. 6:5)
HIS PHRASE	זוג חביב—A beloved partner
HIS BLESSING	His purity of spirit and holy innocence will make him a beloved friend and an exceptional husband.

ZAMIR זָמִיר

HEBREW	A song, a bird
GEMATRIA	257
HIS WORD	נורא—Awesome (Gen. 28:17)
HIS PHRASE	בטובה וברכה—With goodness and blessing
HIS BLESSING	He will bring the joy of music and the beauty of the birds to his surroundings.

ZARACH זרח

HEBREW	Light rising
GEMATRIA	215
HIS WORD	גביר—Lord, ruler (Gen. 27:29)
HIS PHRASE	דיין נאמן—A trustworthy judge
HIS BLESSING	He will shine forth as a leader and be trusted by all.

ZAVDI זבדי

HEBREW	My gift, my gift is God
GEMATRIA	23
HIS WORD	וטוב—And good (Gen. 2:9)
HIS PHRASE	אח אהוב—A beloved brother
HIS BLESSING	He will establish strong familial ties with his friends and be considered a special gift from God.

ZECHARYAH זכריה

VARIANT	Zachariah
HEBREW	Remembrance of God
GEMATRIA	242
HIS WORD	ברכך—Has blessed you (Deut. 2:7)
HIS PHRASE	היה זהיר—Be careful
HIS BLESSING	Scrupulous, careful, and concerned with remembering lessons from the past, he will find blessing.

ZECHER זכר

HEBREW	Memory
GEMATRIA	227
HIS WORD	ברכה—Blessing (Gen. 12:2)
HIS PHRASE	נס ופלא—Miracle and wonder
HIS BLESSING	He will link his life with the great of past generations. He will achieve miracles.

ZEHAVI זהבי

HEBREW	Gold
GEMATRIA	24
HIS WORD	ויאהב—And he loved (Gen. 25:28)
HIS PHRASE	זה הוא—This is the one
HIS BLESSING	He will be the answer to your prayers. He will be unique and special, as precious as gold.

ZEMARIA זמריה

HEBREW	Song, melody of God
GEMATRIA	262
HIS WORD	מברך—Is blessed (Num. 22:6)
HIS PHRASE	קול אהוב וחביב למטה—A beloved and dear voice below
HIS BLESSING	He will be blessed with the ability to sing and to exult in the wonders of God's world.

ZEMER זמר

HEBREW	Song
GEMATRIA	247
HIS WORD	מרבה—Increase (Lev. 11:42)
HIS PHRASE	עסק טוב—Good business
HIS BLESSING	He will constantly increase his blessings of wealth and good fortune. His life will be a song of joy.

ZERA זרע

HEBREW	Seed
GEMATRIA	277
HIS WORD	עזר•—A helpmate (Gen. 2:18)
HIS PHRASE	סימן טוב ומזל טוב—A good sign and good fortune
HIS BLESSING	Together with his children and helpers he will be blessed with exceptional good fortune.

ZERACHYA זרחיה

HEBREW	God shines
GEMATRIA	230
HIS WORD	הטהורה—The pure one (Gen. 7:2)
HIS PHRASE	בזמן הנכון—At the right time
HIS BLESSING	God will shine upon him at an especially appropriate time in his life.

ZERUBAVEL זרובבל

HEBREW	Born in Babylon
GEMATRIA	247
HIS WORD	מרבה—Increasing (Lev. 11:42)
HIS PHRASE	וכל מאמינים—And all believe
HIS BLESSING	He will inspire trust and belief in others. He will increase his blessings with the passage of time.

ZETAN זיתן

HEBREW	Olive tree
GEMATRIA	467
HIS WORD	ויתמהו—And they marveled (Gen. 43:33)
HIS PHRASE	יעשה טוב ולא יחטא—He will do good and not sin
HIS BLESSING	People will stand in awe and wonderment at his goodness and sinlessness.

ZEV זאב

VARIANT	Ze'eiv, Zeev
HEBREW	Deer, wolf
GEMATRIA	10
HIS WORD	בדד—Alone (Lev. 13:46)
HIS PHRASE	גד בא—Good fortune comes
HIS BLESSING	Independent and strong, he will achieve good fortune by himself.

ZEVADIA זבדיה

HEBREW	Gift of the Lord
GEMATRIA	28
HIS WORD	כח—Power, might (Num. 14:17)
HIS PHRASE	יד זהב—A golden hand
HIS BLESSING	He will be strong, able, and artistic.

ZEVUL זבול

HEBREW	Residence
GEMATRIA	45
HIS WORD	מאד—Very much (Gen. 1:33)
HIS PHRASE	ידיד טוב—A good friend
HIS BLESSING	His home will always be open to friends and neighbors.

ZEVULUN זבולון

HEBREW	To exalt, honor, or a lofty house
GEMATRIA	101
HIS WORD	צוה—He commanded (Gen. 6:22)
HIS PHRASE	הדן יחידי—He who judges alone
HIS BLESSING	He will have a commanding presence and an independent spirit.

ZIMRA זמרא

HEBREW	Song
GEMATRIA	248
HIS WORD	לריח—For a pleasant odor (Ex. 29:25)
HIS PHRASE	חפץ בחיים—He desires life
HIS BLESSING	He will love life and enjoy it to the fullest. He will be moved by music, finding special delight in song.

255

ZIMRI זמרי

HEBREW	Mountain sheep, goat, protected sacred thing, my vine, my branch
GEMATRIA	257
HIS WORD	נורא—Awesome (Gen. 28:17)
HIS PHRASE	לו הגבורה—To him is strength
HIS BLESSING	He will be especially protected from all harm. He will find awesome strength within himself in times of need.

ZIV זיו

HEBREW	Brilliant, light, splendor, glory
GEMATRIA	23
HIS WORD	ויז*—And he sprinkled (Lev. 8:11)
HIS PHRASE	האביב בא—Spring has come
HIS BLESSING	Like the splendor of the spring season, he will be the harbinger of much beauty and fulfillment to follow.

ZIVAN זיון

HEBREW	Brilliance, light. Also a synonym for the month of Iyar, the month of the Jewish calendar, in which we celebrate Israel's Independence day.
GEMATRIA	73
HIS WORD	חכמה—Wisdom (Ex. 28:3)
HIS PHRASE	זה היום—This day today
HIS BLESSING	He will fulfill his responsibilities quickly and wisely. He will be extremely sensitive to time and to promptness.

ZOHAR זהר

HEBREW	Light, brilliance
GEMATRIA	212
HIS WORD	זרה*—Strange, different (Ex. 30:9)
HIS PHRASE	לבעלי סוד—To masters of secrets
HIS BLESSING	He will be highly spiritual and attuned to the mystical. He will probe the mysteries of the universe with brilliant insight.

APPENDIX

NAMING A BABY AFTER A RELATIVE— THE MYSTICAL ALTERNATIVE

THE CUSTOM

It has long been a practice to remember loved ones by naming newborn children after them.

Jews of Ashkenazi origin, from Central or Eastern Europe, use only the names of relatives already deceased to be perpetuated. Jews from Spain, Portugal, Italy, North Africa, or the Middle East—known as *sephardim*—observe the custom of naming children even after those who are still alive and deeply beloved.

In either case, giving a name to a newborn in honor of the living or in memory of one who has previously lived is a powerfully spiritual way to link past and future, to connect values of generations before to hopes and aspirations of generations to come, and—in a mystical manner alluded to by our sages—to create a very special bond between two souls now inextricably joined together by virtue of sharing the most precious possession of identity, their very names themselves.

Indeed, tradition teaches us that when a child is named after someone, the original namesake becomes the child's guardian angel, protector, and even intercedor on high.

HOW TO NAME AFTER SOMEONE

Although the simplest way to call a child after someone is to use the very same name, there are many times when this is not practical or feasible. The original name may have been a Yiddish word, a name no longer used, or a name with modern unpleasant connections, or it may have been a name for the opposite gender of the child now to be linked with him or her.

That is why it has become common practice to allow alternative methods for naming a child after another.

1. **Names that share the same letters:** You may look for a name which shares most or many of the letters of the name of the person you seek to remember. For example, the name Zalman, which was common in Yiddish-speaking areas of generations past, may be connected with modern Hebrew names beginning with the same letter *Z* and sharing at least one more letter as well (for example, Zemer or Zivan).

2. **Names that share the same meaning:** You may look for a name which has the same meaning in Hebrew. For example, the girl's name Gitele, extremely common as a Yiddish name that means "good" or "good person," can be expressed by many modern Hebrew names that contain the word *Tov* (good). Some examples include Tovah, Tovit, or even Naamah or Naomi, which all mean pleasantness.

Based on the principle of *gematria* as elucidated in the book, we suggest a third alternative. Since the spiritual key to the essence of the soul is, as we have clarified, implicit in the number total of the name's letters, names that are linked by *gematria*—the same number total—are linked in a most profound way as well as by personality, by proclivity, and by destiny.

For that reason we have added this final portion to this book that will allow you to readily find a name you will be comfortable with in memory or in honor of a loved one, even if you are using female for male or the reverse. Simply find the *gematria* of the name of the person you want to honor and then look for a list of options available under the same number in the pages that follow.

Above all, remember: When your child is old enough to understand, make sure you explain the meaning of his/her name, the reason why this particular name was chosen, and the identity of the person after whom he/she was named.

Hebrew Alphabet,
Transliterations, and Numerical Values

Hebrew Character	Name	Transliteration	Numerical Value
א	Alef	omit	1
בּ,ב	Bet, Vet	b,v	2
ג	Gimel	g	3
ד	Dalet	d	4
ה	He	h	5
ו	Vav	v	6
ז	Zayin	z	7
ח	Het	h	8
ט	Tet	t	9
י	Yod	y	10
כ,כּ	Kaf, Khaf	k, kh	20
ל	Lamed	l	30
מ,ם	Mem	m	40
נ,ן	Num	n	50
ס	Samekh	s	60
ע	Ayin	omit	70
פ,פּ,ף	Pe, Fe	p, f	80
צ	Zade	z	90
ק	Kuf	k	100
ר	Resh	r	200
שׂ,שׁ	Sin, Shin	s, sh	300
ת,תּ	Tav, Sav	t, s	400

ABBA	4	אבא	Boy
DOV	6	דב	Boy
GAD	7	גד	Boy
ZEV, ZE'EIV, ZEEV	10	זאב	Boy
ACHAV	12	אחאב	Boy
GADA	12	גדה	Girl
AVI	13	אבי	Boy
AHAVA	13	אהבה	Girl
GAI	14	גיא	Boy
DOVEV	14	דובב	Boy
DAVID	14	דוד	Boy
AVIV	15	אביב	Boy
HOD	15	הוד	Boy
ADVA	16	אדוה	Girl
EHUD	16	אהוד	Boy
AYA	16	איה	Girl
ADIV	17	אדיב	Boy
GEDI	17	גדי	Boy
DOVA	17	דובה	Girl
AHUVA	19	אהובה	Girl
IYOV	19	איוב	Boy
DODA	19	דודה	Girl
DAYA	19	דיה	Girl
ZEHAVA, ZAHAVA	19	זהבה	Girl
ZAZA	19	זזה	Girl

CHAVA	19	חוה	Girl
YOAV	19	יואב	Boy
DODO	20	דודו	Boy
IDO	21	אידו	Boy
CHAGAI	21	חגי	Boy
ADIVA	22	אדיבה	Girl
TABBAI	22	טבאי	Boy
TOVAH	22	טובה	Girl
ZABDI	23	זבדי	Boy
ZAVDI	23	זבדי	Boy
ZIV	23	זיו	Boy
CHEDVA	23	חדוה	Girl
CHAYA	23	חיה	Girl
ACHIYA	24	אחיה	Boy
DODI	24	דודי	Girl
ZEHAVI	24	זהבי	Boy
GISA, GIZA	25	גיזה	Girl
CHIBA	25	חיבה	Girl
CHAGIYA	26	חגיה	Girl
YATVA	26	יטבה	Girl
CHAVIVA	27	חביבה	Girl
ZEVADIA	28	זבדיה	Boy
ZEVIDA	28	זבידה	Girl
ZIVA	28	זיוה	Girl
YEDID	28	ידיד	Boy

DAVIDA	29	דוידה	Girl
HODAYA	30	הודיה	Boy
HODAYA	30	הודיה	Girl
YEHUDAH	30	יהודה	Boy
AVICHAI	31	אביחי	Boy
ZAKA	32	זכה	Girl
CHABIBI, CHAVIVI	32	חביבי	Boy
TUVYA, TUVYAH	32	טוביה	Boy
LEV	32	לב	Boy
GAL	33	גל	Boy
YEDIDAH, YEDIDA	33	ידידה	Girl
YEHUDI	35	יהודי	Boy
LEAH	36	לאה	Girl
HEVEL	37	הבל	Boy
ZAKKAI	38	זכאי	Boy
TAL	39	טל	Boy
BILDAD	40	בלדד	Boy
GOEL	40	גואל	Boy
HILA	40	הלה	Girl
LEE	40	לי	Boy
LEE	40	לי	Girl
IMMA	42	אמא	Girl
BILHAH	42	בלהה	Girl
YOCHEVED	42	יוכבד	Girl
GADOL	43	גדול	Boy

GIL	43	גיל	Boy
YAGEL	43	יגל	Boy
LAVI	43	לביא	Boy
YIGAL	44	יגאל	Boy
ADAM	45	אדם	Boy
GEULA, GEULAH	45	גאולה	Girl
ZEVUL	45	זבול	Boy
LOT	45	לוט	Boy
AYALAH	46	אילה	Girl
AYLA	46	אילה	Girl
LEVI	46	לוי	Boy
CHULDA	47	חלדה	Girl
YOEL	47	יואל	Boy
LIBA	47	ליבה	Girl
MEGED	47	מגד	Boy
GADIEL	48	גדיאל	Boy
GILA, GILAH	48	גילה	Girl
GALYA, GALIA	48	גליה	Girl
DEGULA	48	דגולה	Girl
YUVAL	48	יובל	Boy
LIVIA	48	לביאה	Girl
AVIELA	49	אביאלה	Girl
DALIA, DALYA	49	דליה	Girl
TALI	49	טלי	Girl
YIGAALA	49	יגאלה	Girl

ZEVULA	50	זבולה	Girl
TALIA	50	טליא	Boy
EDOM	51	אדום	Boy
AYAL	51	אייל	Boy
EYAL	51	אייל	Boy
GOZALA	51	גוזלה	Girl
LEVIA	51	לויה	Girl
AVITAL	52	אביטל	Boy
AVITAL	52	אביטל	Girl
ELIYAHU	52	אליהו	Boy
GEDALYAH, GEDALIA, GEDALYA	52	גדליה	Boy
ZELYA	52	זליה	Girl
YOELA	52	יואלה	Girl
CALEB	52	כלב	Boy
GAN	53	גן	Boy
CHILA	53	חילה	Girl
YAGIL	53	יגיל	Boy
YOVELAH, YOVELA	53	יובלה	Girl
KOCHAVA	53	כוכבה	Girl
DAN	54	דן	Boy
TALI, TALYA, TELI	54	טליה	Girl
YEDIEL	55	ידיאל	Boy
MIA	55	מיה	Girl
NEGEV	55	נגב	Boy
AVIGAIYIL	56	אביגיל	Girl
NADAV, NADAB	56	נדב	Boy

DAGAN	57	דגן	Boy
GANA	58	גנה	Girl
NOAH	58	נח	Boy
YECHIEL	59	יחיאל	Boy
AVICHAYIL	61	אביחיל	Girl
ODEHLIYA	61	אודהליה	Girl
LAEL	61	לאל	Boy
METAV	61	מיטב	Boy
ASA	62	אסא	Boy
NAVA	62	נאוה	Girl
NIV	62	ניב	Boy
BONA	63	בונה	Girl
CHAMUDAH	63	חמודה	Girl
CHAMIYAH	63	חמיה	Boy
CHANNAH	63	חנה	Girl
YECHIELAH, YECHIELA	64	יחיאלה	Girl
NOGA	64	נוגה	Boy
NOGA	64	נוגה	Girl
HILLEL	65	הלל	Boy
NADIV	66	נדיב	Boy
NOY	66	נוי	Boy
NAGID	67	נגיד	Boy
OZNI	68	אזני	Boy
GINA, GENA	68	גינה	Girl
CHAYIM	68	חיים	Boy
AVINADOV	69	אבינדב	Boy

DINA, DINAH	69	דינה	Girl
HADAS	69	הדס	Girl
NUCHA	69	נוחה	Girl
YUDAN	70	יודן	Boy
YONAH	71	יונה	Boy
NEDIVA	71	נדיבה	Girl
NOYA	71	נויה	Girl
DEGANYA	72	דגניה	Girl
YOVIN	72	יבין	Boy
MACCABEE	72	מכבי	Boy
NAGIDA	72	נגידה	Girl
GALIL	73	גליל	Boy
ZIVAN	73	זיון	Boy
CHISDA	73	חסרא	Boy
YOM TOV	73	יום טוב	Boy
MAGAL	73	מגל	Girl
HADASSAH	74	הדסה	Girl
YADIN	74	ידין	Boy
GEVA	75	גבע	Boy
LAILA	75	לילה	Girl
MICHA	75	מיכה	Boy
ADONIYAH	76	אדוניה	Boy
YEHONADAV	77	יהונדב	Boy
MAZAL	77	מזל	Girl
NOYVA, NOVA	77	נויוה	Girl
OZ	77	עז	Boy

GALILA	78	גלילה	Girl
CHALIL	78	חליל	Boy
BOAZ	79	בעז	Boy
DELILA	79	דלילה	Girl
YOHANA, YOCHANA	79	יוחנה	Girl
LITAL	79	ליטל	Girl
GIVA	80	גבעה	Girl
LILY	80	לילי	Girl
ZISSA	82	זיסה	Girl
LAVAN, LABAN	82	לבן	Boy
MIGDALA	82	מגדלה	Girl
OVED, OBED	82	עובד	Boy
AZA	82	עזה	Girl
CHASDAI	83	חסדאי	Boy
CHASYA	83	חסיה	Girl
CHANOCH	84	חנוך	Boy
ADI	84	עדי	Boy
ADI	84	עדי	Girl
ODED	84	עודד	Boy
AVIAD	87	אביעד	Boy
ALON	87	אלון	Boy
ZIA	87	זיע	Girl
CHASIDA	87	חסידה	Girl
LEVANAH	87	לבנה	Girl
AZI	87	עזי	Boy
PAZ	87	פז	Girl

MECHOLA, MEHOLA	89	מחולה	Girl
ADAYA	89	עדיה	Girl
EDYA	89	עדיה	Girl
ODEDA	89	עודדה	Girl
KALIL	90	כליל	Boy
MILI	90	מילי	Girl
ILAN	91	אילן	Boy
ALONA	92	אלונה	Girl
MAGEN	93	מגן	Boy
NACHALAH	93	נחלה	Girl
SEGEL	93	סגל	Boy
UZI	93	עוזי	Boy
MAZAL TOV	94	מזל טוב	Boy
DANIEL	95	דניאל	Boy
YISKAH	95	יסכה	Girl
YAFFAH, YAFFA	95	יפה	Girl
KELILA	95	כלילה	Girl
LOTAN	95	לוטן	Boy
LENA	95	לינה	Girl
MALKA, MALKAH	95	מלכה	Girl
ILANA	96	אילנה	Girl
AMANA, AMANAH	96	אמנה	Girl
EILON	97	אילון	Boy
OBEDIAH, OBADIAH	97	עובדיה	Boy
OVADYA	97	עובדיה	Boy
SOVEL, SOBEL	98	סובל	Girl

AZIZA	99	עזיזה	Girl
DANIELLA	100	דניאלה	Girl
MICHAL	100	מיכל	Girl
NILI	100	נילי	Boy
NILI	100	נילי	Girl
ADMON	101	אדמון	Boy
ZEVULUN	101	זבולון	Boy
MICHAEL	101	מיכאל	Boy
MALACHI	101	מלאכי	Boy
EMUNAH	102	אמונה	Girl
LEONA	102	ליאונה	Girl
MIGDANA	102	מגדנה	Girl
PAZIA	102	פזיה	Girl
TZEVI, TZVI	102	צבי	Boy
AVIMELECH	103	אבימלך	Boy
YAVNIEL	103	יבניאל	Boy
NECHAMA	103	נחמה	Girl
SIGAL	103	סיגל	Girl
ELAD	105	אלעד	Boy
YEMIMAH, YEMIMA	105	ימימה	Girl
MINA, MENA	105	מינה	Girl
NIMA, NEMA	105	נימה	Girl
ADMONA	106	ארמונה	Girl
MICHAELA	106	מיכאלה	Girl
GILAD	107	גלעד	Boy
TZIVYAH	107	צביה	Girl

CHANAN	108	חנן	Boy
NAVON	108	נבון	Boy
BAZAK	109	בזק	Boy
DITZA	109	דיצה	Girl
MENUCHA	109	מנוחה	Girl
MASADA	109	מסדה	Girl
YAEL	110	יעל	Girl
ELI	110	עלי	Boy
PIYUTA	110	פיוטה	Girl
GILADA	112	גלעדה	Girl
NECHEMYA	113	נחמיה	Boy
AVUKA	114	אבוקה	Girl
GAMLIEL	114	גמליאל	Boy
YEMINAH, YEMINA	115	ימינה	Girl
NISA	115	נסה	Girl
SIMA	115	סימה	Girl
ILLA	115	עילה	Girl
ALIYA	115	עליה	Girl
ALUF, ALUPH	117	אלוף	Boy
NEGINA	118	נגינה	Girl
AMI	120	עמי	Boy
YONANAH	121	יונה	Girl
ALUFA	122	אלופה	Girl
ZILPAH	122	זלפה	Girl
ALIZA	122	עליזה	Girl
CHANANIA	123	חנניה	Boy

YOHANAN	124	יוחנן	Boy
EDEN	124	עדן	Boy
EDEN	124	עדן	Girl
UZZIEL	124	עוזיאל	Boy
NASIA	125	נסיה	Girl
SIVAN	126	סיון	Boy
NETA	129	נטע	Girl
PALTI	129	פלטי	Boy
CHIZKIYA	130	חזקיה	Boy
NODA	130	נודע	Boy
SINAI	130	סיני	Boy
ELIMELECH	131	אלימלך	Boy
AMATZ	131	אמץ	Boy
GIVON	131	גבעון	Boy
GIDEON	133	גדעון	Boy
CHASINA	133	חסינה	Girl
DEKEL	134	דקל	Boy
LETIFA	134	לטיפה	Girl
IDAN	134	עידן	Boy
TZILLA	135	צילה	Girl
CHIZKIYAHU	136	חזקיהו	Boy
TIBON	137	טבעון	Boy
GAFNA	138	גפנה	Girl
MENACHEM	138	מנחם	Boy
AMICHAI	138	צמיחי	Boy
TZEMACH	138	עמח	Boy

ELCHANAN, ELHANAN	139	אלחנן	Boy
DAFNA	139	דפנה	Girl
DAPHNE	139	דפנה	Girl
DICKLA	139	דקלה	Girl
ADINA	139	עדינה	Girl
ASAF, ASAPH	141	אסף	Boy
TIVONA	142	טבעונה	Girl
MENACHEMA	143	מנחמה	Girl
KEDEM	144	קדם	Boy
MATMON	145	מטמון	Boy
NITZA	145	נצה	Girl
ALMA	145	עלמה	Girl
AMIZA, AMITZA	146	אמיצה	Girl
AMNON	147	אמנון	Boy
GEFANIA	148	גפניה	Boy
CHOFNI, CHAFNI	148	חפני	Boy
NACHMAN	148	נחמן	Boy
PESACH	148	פסח	Boy
SAADYA	149	סעדיה	Boy
KEDMA	149	קדמה	Girl
EILAM	150	עילם	Boy
NOFIA	151	נופיה	Girl
AMIEL	151	עמיאל	Boy
INBAL	152	ענבל	Girl
BETZALEIL, BETZALEL	153	בצלאל	Boy
CHILKIYA	153	חלקיה	Boy

LAADAN	154	לעדן	Boy
AMALIA	155	עמליה	Girl
YOSEF	156	יוסף	Boy
YECHEZKIEL	156	יחזקאל	Boy
TZION	156	ציון	Boy
MANGENA	158	מנגינה	Girl
NISSIM	160	נסים	Boy
YOSEPHA	161	יוספה	Girl
PUAH	161	פועה	Girl
TZIYONA	161	ציונה	Girl
BENJAMIN, BENYAMIN	162	בנימין	Boy
NAAMAH	165	נעמה	Girl
ELIANA	166	אליענה	Girl
MAON	166	מעון	Boy
NOAR	166	נועם	Boy
NISSAN	170	ניסן	Boy
NAAMI, NAOMI	170	נעמי	Girl
ANAN	170	ענן	Boy
BEN-AMI	172	בן-עמי	Boy
AVINOAM	173	בינעם	Boy
AMOS	176	עמוס	Boy
AMINADAV	176	עמינדב	Boy
MATZLIACH	178	מצליח	Boy
MAYAN	180	מעיין	Girl
YEHOYAKIM	181	יהויקים	Boy
YAAKOV, YAKOV	182	יעקב	Boy

AKIVA, AKIBA	183	עקיבא	Boy
ACHINOAM	185	אחינועם	Boy
KADMIEL	185	קדמיאל	Boy
ELKANAH	186	אלקנה	Boy
YACOBA, YACOVA	187	יעקבה	Girl
ELYAKIM, ELIAKIM	191	אליקים	Boy
TZOPHIYAH	191	צופיה	Girl
KANIEL	191	קניאל	Boy
CHEFTZIBAH	195	חפציבה	Girl
PENINA, PENINAH	195	פנינה	Girl
EMANUEL	197	עמנואל	Boy
PINCHAS	198	פנחס	Boy
NITZAN	200	ניצן	Boy
PENINI	200	פניני	Boy
TZADOK	200	צדוק	Boy
EMANUELA	202	עמנואלה	Girl
DAR	204	דר	Boy
KETIFA	204	קטיפה	Girl
ADAR	205	אדר	Boy
ARAD	205	ארד	Boy
NITZANA	205	ניצנה	Girl
ASISA	205	עסיסה	Girl
BARA	207	ברה	Girl
AVIRA	208	אברה	Girl
BEN-TZIYON	208	בן-ציון	Boy
HAGAR	208	הגר	Girl

YITZCHAK	208	יצחק	Boy
HADAR	209	הדר	Boy
HADAR	209	הדר	Girl
DOR	210	דור	Boy
VERED	210	ורד	Boy
VERED	210	ורד	Girl
NAAMAN	210	נעמן	Boy
KENAN	210	קינן	Boy
ARI	211	ארי	Boy
GIBOR	211	גבור	Boy
GOVER	211	גובר	Boy
ORA	212	אורה	Girl
ZOHAR	212	זהר	Boy
ABIR	213	אביר	Boy
HADARA, HADERA	214	הדרה	Girl
CHUR	214	חור	Boy
RAVIV	214	רביב	Boy
ADIR	215	אדיר	Boy
DURA	215	דורה	Girl
VARDA, VARDIA	215	ורדה	Girl
ZARACH	215	זרח	Boy
MITZPA	215	מצפה	Girl
TZIDKIYAHU	215	צדקיהו	Boy
ARYEH, ARYE, ARYEIH	216	אריה	Boy
DEVIR	216	דביר	Boy
CHAVAKUK	216	חבקוק	Boy

RAVID	216	רביד	Boy
URI	217	אורי	Boy
BIRA	217	בירה	Girl
DEVORA, DEVORAH	217	דבורה	Girl
RIVA	217	ריבה	Girl
AVIRA	218	אבירה	Girl
BERIAH	218	בריאה	Boy
ZOHAR	218	זוהר	Girl
ADIRA	220	אדירה	Girl
GEVIRA	220	גבירה	Girl
GEYORA	220	גיורא	Boy
YAIR	221	יאיר	Boy
YORA	221	יורה	Boy
BEHIRA	222	בהירה	Girl
ZIRA	222	זירה	Girl
AVIDOR	223	אבידור	Boy
GAYORA	224	גיורה	Girl
TIRA	224	טירה	Girl
RECHAVIA	225	רחביה	Boy
AVIGDOR	226	אביגדור	Boy
GIBORA, GIVORA	226	גיבורה	Girl
YEIRA	226	יאירה	Girl
ETZYON	226	עציון	Boy
BRACHA	227	ברכה	Girl
ZEHIRA	227	זהירה	Girl
ZECHER	227	זכר	Boy

BARUCH	228	ברוך	Boy
ZARIZA	229	זריזה	Girl
ZERACHYA	230	זרחיה	Boy
AREL	232	אראל	Boy
BECHORA	233	בכורה	Girl
BAREL	233	בר-אל	Boy
ELRAD	235	אלרד	Boy
TZEFANYAH	235	צפניה	Boy
HAREL	236	הראל	Boy
ARELA, ARELLA	237	אראלה	Girl
ERELA	237	אראלה	Girl
BEREKHYAH	237	ברכיה	Boy
RACHEL	238	רחל	Girl
NANA, NAANA	240	נענע	Girl
RAM	240	רם	Boy
ROM	240	רם	Boy
ARIEL	242	אריאל	Boy
ARIELLE	242	אריאל	Girl
ZECHARYAH	242	זכריה	Boy
AMBER	243	אמבר	Girl
REGEM	243	רגם	Boy
RAMA	245	רמה	Girl
GAVRIEL	246	גבריאל	Boy
TALOR	246	טלאור	Boy
TALOR	246	טלאור	Girl
ORLEE	247	אורלי	Girl

ARIELA	247	אריאלה	Girl
ZEMER	247	זמר	Boy
ZERUBAVEL	247	זרובבל	Boy
LEOR	247	ליאור	Boy
MAOR	247	מאור	Boy
AVRAHAM	248	אברהם	Boy
URIEL	248	אוריאל	Boy
GIMRA	248	גמרה	Girl
ZIMRA	248	זמרא	Boy
BARZILAI	249	ברזלי	Boy
GOMER	249	גומר	Boy
GOMER	249	גומר	Girl
GURIEL	250	גוריאל	Boy
RON	250	רן	Boy
AMIR	251	אמיר	Boy
IMRI	251	אמרי	Boy
GAVRIELA	251	גבריאלה	Girl
DURIEL	251	דוריאל	Boy
MEIR	251	מאיר	Boy
MARVA	251	מרוה	Girl
ORAHLEE	252	אורהלי	Girl
ZIMRA	252	זמרה	Girl
LEORA	252	ליאורה	Girl
AVIRAM	253	אבירם	Boy
AVNER	253	אבנר	Boy
URIELA	253	אוריאלה	Girl

ELIORA	253	אליאורה	Girl
RACHAMA	253	רחמה	Girl
MAHIR	255	מהיר	Boy
MAXIMA	255	מקסימה	Girl
RAVITAL	255	רויטל	Girl
AHARON	256	אהרן	Boy
AMIRA	256	אמירה	Girl
ORNA	256	ארנה	Girl
YORAM	256	יורם	Boy
MEIRA	256	מאירה	Girl
NUR	256	נור	Boy
ATZMON	256	עצמון	Boy
OREN	257	אורן	Boy
ZAMIR	257	זמיר	Boy
ZIMRI	257	זמרי	Boy
NAOR	257	נאור	Boy
RAZILEE	257	רזילי	Girl
CHIRAM	258	חירם	Boy
GOREN	259	גורן	Boy
REUVEN, REUBEN	259	ראובן	Boy
MAHIRA	260	מהירה	Girl
NIR	260	ניר	Boy
AMIKAM	260	עמיקם	Boy
RANI	260	רני	Girl
AHARONA	261	אהרנה	Girl
ARDON	261	ארדון	Boy

MORIA	261	מוריה	Girl
ROMIA	261	רומיה	Girl
ZEMARIA	262	זמריה	Boy
NEORA	262	נאורה	Girl
YARDAN	264	ירדן	Boy
YERUCHAM	264	ירוחם	Boy
KARMA	265	כרמה	Girl
NAHIR	265	נהיר	Boy
NIRA	265	נירה	Girl
RINA, RENA	265	רינה	Girl
DORON	266	דורון	Boy
YORON	266	יורן	Boy
YARON	266	ירון	Boy
YARDENAH	269	ירדנה	Girl
DORIN	270	דורין	Girl
ER	270	ער	Boy
ASIR	271	אסיר	Boy
DORONA	271	דורונה	Girl
YIRMIYAHU	271	ירמיהו	Boy
EIVER	272	עבר	Boy
MORDECHAI	274	מרדכי	Boy
GURION	275	גוריון	Boy
KETZIA	275	קציעה	Girl
ZERA	277	זרע	Boy
ARAVA	277	ערבה	Girl
EZRA	278	עזרא	Boy

ERGA	278	ערגה	Girl
YAAR	280	יער	Boy
IVRI	282	עברי	Boy
IVRI	282	עברי	Girl
EZRA	282	עזרה	Girl
OZER	283	עוזר	Boy
ATARA	284	עטרה	Girl
RAYA	285	רעיה	Girl
OFRAH, OPRAH	286	אפרה	Girl
MAROM	286	מרום	Boy
MORIEL	287	מוריאל	Girl
RACHMIEL	289	רחמיאל	Boy
AVIEZER	290	אביעזר	Boy
CARMEL, CARMI	290	כרמל	Boy
LIRON	290	לירן	Boy
MIRIAM	290	מרים	Girl
ATURA	290	עטורה	Girl
PERI	290	פרי	Girl
AZARYAH	292	עזריה	Boy
YEPHRA	295	יפרה	Girl
CARMELA	295	כרמלה	Girl
ACHIEZER	296	אחיעזר	Boy
MORAN	296	מורן	Boy
RIMON	296	רמון	Boy
ARMON	297	ארמון	Boy
RACHAMIM	298	רחמים	Boy

YERACHMIEL	299	ירחמיאל	Boy
FREIDA, FRIEDA	299	פרידה	Girl
RANEN	300	רנן	Boy
LIRONA	301	לירונה	Girl
MENORA	301	מנורה	Girl
PORIYAH	301	פוריה	Girl
PRIVA	301	פריוה	Girl
RIMONA	301	רמונה	Girl
BARAK	302	ברק	Boy
ZEFIRAH	302	זפירה	Girl
KALONYMUS	302	קלונימוס	Boy
PERACHYA	303	פרחיה	Girl
SMADAR	304	סמדר	Girl
SEGEV	305	שׂגב	Boy
MERON	306	מירון	Boy
ARNON	307	ארנון	Boy
RE'UEL	307	רעואל	Boy
RIVKA, RIVKAH	307	רבקה	Girl
ELAZAR	308	אלעזר	Boy
CHERMONA	309	חרמונה	Girl
SHEVACH	310	שבח	Boy
SHAI	310	שי	Boy
DIVSHA	311	דבשה	Girl
RAPHAEL, RAFAEL	311	רפאל	Boy
BARAM	312	ברעם	Boy
KEFIRA	315	כפירה	Girl

ADRIEL	315	עדריאל	Boy
RAPHAELA	316	רפאלה	Girl
ELIEZER	318	אליעזר	Boy
AZRIEL	318	עזריאל	Boy
YAKIR	320	יקיר	Boy
YISHAI	320	ישי	Boy
OMRI	320	חמרי	Boy
ERAN	320	ערן	Boy
YEHOASH	322	יהואש	Boy
YAKIRA	325	יקירה	Girl
NAARA	325	נערה	Girl
EVENEZER	330	אבנעזר	Boy
EFRAYIM, EPHRAIM	331	אפרים	Boy
YOSHIYAH	331	יושיה	Boy
CLARA	335	קלרה	Girl
TZURIEL	337	צוריאל	Boy
SHAUL	337	שאול	Boy
HERTZLIYA	340	הרצליה	Girl
SHULA	341	שולה	Girl
SHALVA, SHALVAH	341	שלוה	Girl
TARPHON	345	טרפון	Boy
MOSHE	345	משה	Boy
MASHA	345	משה	Girl
RICKMA	345	רקמה	Girl
MARNIN	350	מרנין	Boy
KEREN	350	קרן	Boy

KEREN	350	קרן	Girl
CARNA	351	קרנא	Girl
SHOAM	351	שוהם	Boy
SHAMAI	351	שמאי	Boy
SHEVNA	353	שבנא	Boy
SIMCHA	353	שמחה	Boy
SIMCHA	353	שמחה	Girl
MARNINA	355	מרנינה	Girl
AFRA	355	עפרה	Girl
ORPAH	355	ערפה	Girl
OFER	356	עופר	Boy
KOREN	356	קורן	Boy
ENOSH	357	אנוש	Boy
ESHKOL	357	אשכול	Boy
AMIRAM	360	עמירם	Boy
ALEKSANDER, ALEXANDER	365	אלכסנדר	Boy
OPHIRA	365	עפירה	Girl
YARKON	366	ירקון	Boy
ELINOAR	367	אלינוער	Girl
LESHEM	370	לשם	Boy
PERETZ	370	פרץ	Boy
RAANAN	370	רענן	Boy
YARKANAH	371	ירקונה	Girl
SHEBA	372	שבע	Girl
RANANA	375	רעננה	Girl
SHLOMOH	375	שלמה	Boy

SHALOM	376	שלום	Boy
SHMUEL, SAMUEL	377	שמואל	Boy
AVSHALOM	379	אבשלום	Boy
HOSHEA	381	הושע	Boy
TZIPPORAH	381	צפורה	Girl
ZEPHIRAH	385	צפירה	Girl
SHACHANYAH	385	שכניה	Boy
YEHOSHUA	391	יהושע	Boy
MENASHEH	395	מנשה	Boy
NESHAMA	395	נשמה	Girl
KARNIELA	396	קרניאלה	Girl
MASKIL	400	משכיל	Boy
YESHAYAHU, YESHAIYAHU	401	ישעיהו	Boy
SHAANAN	401	שאנן	Boy
TAGA	408	תגה	Girl
DEROR	410	דרור	Boy
SHAMA	410	שמע	Boy
ELISHA	411	אלישע	Boy
ITI, ITTI	411	אתי	Girl
EFRONA	411	עפרונה	Girl
ELISHEVA	413	אלישבע	Girl
GITAI	413	גתי	Boy
NACHSHON	414	נחשון	Boy
DERORA	415	דבורה	Girl
ETYA	416	אתיה	Girl
MESHULAM	416	משולם	Boy

BATYA	417	בתיה	Girl
ZAYIT	417	זית	Girl
SHLUMIEIL	417	שלומיאל	Boy
DASIA	419	דתיה	Girl
GAZIT	420	גזית	Girl
SHALMAN	420	שלמן	Boy
CHAGIT	421	חגית	Girl
ZETA	422	זיתה	Girl
BRURIA, BERURIYA	423	ברוריה	Girl
TECHIYA	423	תחיה	Girl
SHMAYAH	425	שמעיה	Boy
SHEMAYAHU	431	שמעיהו	Boy
BAT-EL	433	בת-אל	Girl
BET-EL, BETHEL	433	בתאל	Girl
YEHUDIS, YEHUDIT	435	יהודית	Girl
AYELET	441	אילת	Girl
EMMET	441	אמת	Boy
LEEAT, LIAT	441	ליאת	Girl
DALICE, DALIT	444	דלית	Girl
AMITA	446	אמתה	Girl
TE'OM (THOMAS)	447	תאום	Boy
ALEXANDRA	450	אלקסנדרה	Girl
TEHILLAH	450	תהילה	Girl
AMMITAI	451	אמתי	Boy
YISHMAEL	451	ישמעאל	Boy
ITIEL	452	איתיאל	Boy

DOSON, DOTON	454	דתן	Boy
DATAN	454	דתן	Boy
ATNA	456	אתנה	Girl
YOTAM	456	יותם	Boy
BAT-CHEN	460	בת-חן	Girl
EITAN	461	איתן	Boy
GINAS, GINAT	463	גינת	Girl
GANIT	463	גנית	Girl
ETANA	466	איתנה	Girl
SHIMON	466	שמעון	Boy
DEGANIT	467	דגנית	Girl
ZETAN	467	זיתן	Boy
CHANIT	468	חנית	Girl
TALMA	475	תלמה	Girl
TALMAI	480	תלמי	Boy
MATILDA	489	מתילדה	Girl
ATIDA	489	עתידה	Girl
YEFES, YEFET	490	יפת	Boy
MATAN	490	מתן	Boy
AMITAN	491	אמתן	Boy
IDIT	494	עידית	Girl
MATANA	495	מתנה	Girl
TEMIMA	495	תמימה	Girl
YIFTOCH	498	יפתח	Boy
NATAN	500	נתן	Boy
TEMAN	500	תימן	Boy

ASHER	501	אשר	Boy
SHERAGA	504	שרגא	Boy
TANCHUM	504	תנחום	Boy
SARA	505	ערה	Girl
SHACHAR	508	שחר	Girl
GINSON, GINTON	509	גנתון	Boy
KALANIT	510	כלנית	Girl
TIKVAH	511	תקוה	Girl
NATANIA	515	נתניה	Girl
ATALYA	515	עתליה	Girl
SHIRA	515	שירה	Girl
YONATAN	516	יונתן	Boy
AVISHUR	519	אבישור	Boy
ILIT	520	עילית	Girl
ANAT	520	ענת	Girl
YEHONASAN, YEHONATAN	521	יהונתן	Boy
YERUSHA	521	ירושה	Girl
KORESH	526	כורש	Boy
LAPIDOS, LAPIDOT	530	לפידות	Boy
EINAT	530	עינת	Girl
NATHANIEL, NATANEL	531	נתנאל	Boy
SHLOM-TZIYON	532	שלם-ציון	Girl
YISRAEL	541	ישראל	Boy
SHIMRA	545	שמרה	Girl
YISRAELA	546	ישראלה	Girl
MATOK	546	מתוק	Boy

GERSHOM	549	גרשום	Boy
SHAMIR	550	שמיר	Boy
MORASHA	551	מורשה	Girl
METUKA	551	מתוקה	Girl
SHARON	556	שרון	Girl
YEKUTIEL	557	יקותיאל	Boy
BAT-ZION	558	בת-ציון	Girl
KANIT	560	קנית	Girl
SHMARYAHU	561	שמריהו	Boy
BAT ZIONA	563	בת ציונה	Girl
SHNEIOR	567	שניאור	Boy
NAMIT	570	נעמית	Girl
NAFTALI	570	נפתלי	Boy
YESHURUN	572	ישורון	Boy
SHEFER	580	שפר	Boy
ASHIRA	585	עשירה	Girl
SHAPIR	590	שפיר	Boy
SHIFRA	595	שיפרה	Girl
ADERET	605	אדרת	Girl
RUTH	606	רוח	Girl
TIRZAH	612	תרזה	Girl
URIT	617	אורית	Girl
ZOHERET	618	זוהרת	Girl
GURICE, GURIT	619	גורית	Girl
DORIT, DORRIT	620	דורית	Girl
SISI	620	שישי	Boy

YESHISHA	625	יששה	Girl
KITRA	625	כתרה	Girl
YORIT	626	יורית	Girl
AVIRIT	627	אוירית	Girl
ALTER	631	אלתר	Boy
TAMAR, TAMARA	640	תמר	Girl
MARTA	645	מרתה	Girl
TOMER	646	תומר	Boy
LIRIT	650	לירית	Girl
TAMIR	650	תמיר	Boy
ITTAMAR	651	איתמר	Boy
TIMORA	651	תמורה	Girl
TERUMA	651	תרומה	Girl
TEMIRA	655	תמירה	Girl
MORIT	656	מורית	Girl
SHUSHAN	656	שושן	Boy
SASSON	656	ששון	Boy
ESTHER	661	אסתר	Girl
KASRIEL, KATRIEL	661	כתריאל	Boy
SHOSHANA	661	שושנה	Girl
GARNIT	663	גרנית	Girl
ASTERA	666	אסתרה	Girl
NURIT	666	נורית	Girl
RONIT	666	רונית	Girl
ARONIT	667	ארונית	Girl
KINNERET	670	כנרת	Girl

NIRIT	670	נירית	Girl
ATAR	670	עתר	Boy
KITRON	676	כתרון	Boy
RE'UT	676	רעות	Girl
TALMOR	676	תלמור	Girl
BARTHOLOMEW	682	ברתלמי	Boy
MARGOLIT	683	מרגלית	Girl
ATIRA	685	עתירה	Girl
IRIS, IRIT	690	עירית	Girl
TIRTZA	695	תרצה	Girl
SHIMSHON	696	שמשון	Boy
KERET	700	קרת	Girl
SHAYS, SETH	700	שת	Boy
MATRONA	701	מתרונה	Girl
MARGANIT	703	מרגנית	Girl
SHERIRA	711	שרירא	Boy
SHABTAI	713	שבתאי	Boy
SAGIT	713	שגית	Girl
KESHISHA	715	קשישה	Girl
EFRATA	755	עפרתה	Girl
KORENET	756	קורנת	Girl
BATSHEVA	774	בת שבע	Girl
METHUSELAH	784	מתושלח	Boy
SHULAMIT	786	שולמית	Girl
SHLOMIT	786	שלומית	Girl
KESHET	800	קשת	Boy

KESHET	800	קֶשֶׁת	Girl
YISSACHAR	830	יששכר	Boy
MATTISYAHU, MATTATHIAS	861	מתתיהו	Boy
SARIT	910	שרית	Girl
TESHURA	911	תשורה	Girl
ATERET	1070	עתרת	Girl

ALPHABETICAL
LIST OF NAMES

FEMININE NAMES

Abiela (*see* Aviela)

Abigail (*see* Avigaiyil)

Abira (*see* Avira)

Abital (*see* Avital)

Abra (*see* Avira)

Adaya, 17

Aderet, 17

Adi, 17

Adina, 18

Adira, 18

Adiva, 18

Admona, 18

Adva, 19

Afra, 19

Aharona, 19

Ahava, 19

Ahuva, 20

Alexandra, 20

Aliya, 20

Aliza, 20

Alma, 21

Alona, 21

Alufa, 21

Amalia, 21

Amana, Amanah, 22

Amber, 22

Amira, 22

Amisa (*see* Amita)

Amita, 22

Amiza, Amitza, 23

Anat, 23

Arava, 23

Arela, Arella, 23

Ariela, 24

Arielle, 24

Arna (*see* Orna)

Arona (*see* Aharona)

Aronit, 24

Ashira, 24

Asisa, 25

Astera, 25

Atalya, 25

Atara, 25

Ateret, 26

Daphne, 42
Dasia, 42
Datya (*see* Dasia)
Davida, 42
Daya, 43
Deganit, 43
Deganya, 43
Degula, 43
Delila, 44
Derora, 44
Devora, Devorah, 44
Dickla, 44
Dina, Dinah, 45
Ditza, 45
Divsha, 45
Diza (*see* Ditza)
Doba (*see* Dova)
Doda, 45
Dodi, 46
Dorin, 46
Dorit, Dorrit, 46
Dorona, 46
Dova, 47
Dura, 47
Eden, 48
Edya, 48
Efrata, 48
Efrona, 49
Einat, 49
Eitana (*see* Etana)
Elana (*see* Ilana)
Eliana, 49

Elinoar, 49
Eliora, 50
Elisheva, 50
Emanuela, 50
Emunah, 50
Erela, 51
Erga, 51
Esther, 51
Etana, 51
Etya, 52
Ezra, 52
Freida, Frieda, 53
Gabriela (*see* Gavriela)
Gada, 54
Gafna, 54
Galila, 54
Galia (*see* Galya)
Galya, 55
Gana, 55
Ganit, 55
Garnit, 55
Gavriela, 56
Gayora, 56
Gazit, 56
Gena (*see* Gina)
Geula, Geulah, 56
Gevira, 57
Gibora, Givora, 57
Gila, Gilah, 57
Gilada, 57
Gimra, 58
Gina, 58

Ginas, Ginat, 58
Giora (see Gayora)
Gisa, 58
Giva, 59
Giza (see Gisa)
Gomer, 59
Gozala, 59
Gurice, Gurit, 59
Hadar, 60
Hadara, Hadera, 60
Hadas, 60
Hadassah, 61
Hagar, 61
Hagit (see Chagit)
Hagiya (see Chagiya)
Hamuda (see Chamudah)
Hanit (see Chanit)
Hannah (see Channah)
Hasida (see Chasida)
Hasina (see Chasina)
Hasya (see Chasya)
Hava (see Chava)
Haviva (see Chaviva)
Haya (see Chaya)
Hedva (see Chedva)
Heftzibah (see Cheftzibah)
Hermona (see Chermona)
Hertzliya, 61
Hiba (see Chiba)
Hila, 61
Hodaya, 62
Hulda (see Chulda)

Idit, 63
Ilana, 63
Ilit, 63
Illa, 64
Imma, 64
Inbal, 64
Iris, 64
Irit (see Iris)
Israela (see Yisraela)
Iti, Itti, 65
Ivri, 65
Jael (see Yael)
Joanne (see Yohana)
Joela (see Yoela)
Johana (see Yohana)
Jordana (see Yardenah)
Jorit (see Yorit)
Kalanit, 66
Kanit, 66
Karen (see Keren)
Karma, 66
Karna (see Carna)
Karniela, 67
Kassia (see Ketzia)
Kedma, 67
Kefira, 67
Kelila, 67
Keren, 68
Keret, 68
Keshet, 68
Keshisha, 68
Ketifa, 69

Ketzia, 69
Kinneret, 69
Kitra, 69
Kochava, 70
Korenet, 70
Laila, 71
Leah, 71
Leba (see Liba)
Lee, 71
Leeat, 72
Leila (see Laila)
Lena, 72
Leona, 72
Leora, 72
Letifa, 73
Letipha (see Letifa)
Levanah, 73
Levia, 73
Leya (see Leah)
Liba, 73
Liat (see Leeat)
Lieba (see Liba)
Lily, 74
Liora (see Leora)
Lirit, 74
Lirona, 74
Lital, 74
Livia, 75
Liviya (see Livia)
Magal, 76
Mahira, 76
Malka, Malkah, 76

Mangena, 77
Margalit (see Margolit)
Marganit, 77
Margolit, 77
Marnina, 77
Marsa (see Marta)
Marta, 78
Martha (see Marta)
Marva, 78
Masada, 78
Masha, 78
Mashe (see Masha)
Matana, 79
Matilda, 79
Matrona, 79
Maxima, 79
Mayan, 80
Mazal, 80
Mechola, 80
Mehira (see Mahira)
Mehola (see Mechola)
Meira, 80
Mena (see Mina)
Menachema, 81
Menora, 81
Menucha, 81
Metuka, 81
Mia, 82
Michaela, 82
Michal, 82
Migdala, 82
Migdana, 83

MASCULINE NAMES

Aaron (*see* Aharon)

Abba, 135

Abir, 135

Abishur (*see* Avishur)

Abner (*see* Avner)

Abraham (*see* Avraham)

Absalom (*see* Avshalom)

Achav, 135

Achiezer, 136

Achinoam, 136

Achiya, 136

Adam, 136

Adar, 137

Adi, 137

Adir, 137

Adiv, 137

Admon, 138

Adoniyah, 138

Adriel, 138

Ahab (*see* Achav)

Aharon, 138

Akiba (*see* Akiva)

Akiva, 139

Aleksander, 139

Alexander (*see* Aleksander)

Alon, 139

Alter, 139

Aluf, Aluph, 140

Amatz, 140

Ami, 140

Amichai, 140

Amiel, 141

Amikam, 141

Aminadav, 141

Amir, 141

Amiram, 142

Amitan, 142

Ammitai, 142

Amnon, 142

Amos, 143

Anan, 143

Arad, 143

Ardon, 143

Arel, 144

Chisda, 159

Chizkiya, 160

Chizkiyahu, 160

Chofni, 160

Chur, 160

Cyrus (*see* Koresh)

Dagan, 161

Dan, 161

Danieil (*see* Daniel)

Daniel, 161

Daniyel (*see* Daniel)

Danny (*see* Daniel)

Dar, 162

Datan, 162

David, 162

Dekel, 162

Deror, 163

Devir, 163

Dodo, 163

Dor, 163

Doron, 164

Doson, 164

Doton (*see* Doson)

Dov, 164

Dovev, 164

Dror (*see* Deror)

Duriel, 165

Ebenezer (*see* Evenezer)

Eden, 166

Edom, 166

Efrayim, 166

Ehud, 167

Eilam, 167

Eilon, 167

Eitan, 167

Eiver, 168

Elad, 168

Elazar, 168

Elchanan, Elhanan, 168

Eli, 169

Eliakim (*see* Elyakim)

Eliezer, 169

Elimelech, 169

Elisha, 169

Eliyahu, 170

Elkanah, 170

Elrad, 170

Elyakim, 170

Emanuel, 171

Emmet, 171

Enoch (*see* Chanoch)

Enosh, 171

Ephraim (*see* Efrayim)

Er, 171

Eran, 172

Eshkol, 172

Etzyon, 172

Evenezer, 172

Eyal, 173

Ezra, 173

Gabriel (*see* Gavriel)

Gad, 174

Gadi (*see* Gad)

Gadiel, 174

Yadin, 238

Yagel, 239

Yagil, 239

Yair, 239

Yakir, 239

Yardan, 240

Yarkon, 240

Yaron, 240

Yavniel, 240

Yechezkiel, 241

Yechiel, 241

Yedid, 241

Yediel, 241

Yefes, Yefet, 242

Yehoash, 242

Yehonadav, 242

Yehonasan, Yehonatan, 242

Yehoshua, 243

Yehoyakim, 243

Yehudah, 243

Yehudi, 243

Yekutiel, 244

Yerachmiel, 244

Yerucham, 244

Yeshaiyahu (see Yeshayahu)

Yeshayahu, 244

Yeshurun, 245

Yiftoch, 245

Yigal, 245

Yirmiyahu, 245

Yishai, 246

Yishmael, 246

Yisrael, 246

Yissachar, 246

Yitzchak, 247

Yoav, 247

Yoel, 247

Yohanan, 247

Yom Tov, 248

Yonah, 248

Yonatan, 248

Yora, 248

Yoram, 249

Yoron, 249

Yosef, 249

Yoshiyah, 249

Yotam, 250

Yovin, 250

Yudan, 250

Yuval, 250

Zabdi, 251

Zachariah (see Zecharyah)

Zakkai, 251

Zamir, 251

Zarach, 252

Zavdi, 252

Zecharyah, 252

Zecher, 252

Ze'eiv (see Zev)

Zeev (see Zev)

Zehavi, 253

Zemaria, 253

Zemer, 253

Zera, 253

About the Authors

Rabbi Benjamin Blech is a professor of Talmud at Yeshiva University and an internationally recognized educator, religious leader, author, and lecturer. A recipient of the American Educator of the Year Award, Blech has authored 13 highly acclaimed books with combined sales of over a half million copies, including *The Complete Idiot's Guide to Understanding Judaism* and *Understanding Judaism: The Basics of Deed and Creed*. He writes regularly for major newspapers and journals and was recently ranked #16 in a listing of the 50 most influential Jews in America. *Your Name Is Your Blessing* represents Rabbi Blech's first book-length collaboration with his wife, **Elaine**, who has always shared his interest in Jewish scholarship and mysticism.